I.   INTRODUCTION

Certain it is that a great responsibility rests upon the statesmen of all nations, not only to fulfill the promises for reduction in armaments, but to maintain the confidence of the people of the world in the hope of an enduring peace. (Kellogg, 1929)

States are developing cyber weapons. Cyber weapons can target systems anywhere around the world because we have a global interconnected network. Industrialized and developing states dependence on cyberspace and the Internet have turned these tools into "global commons" (Giesen, 2013); however, these tools also provide the conduits for attacks. Any state can target the military organizations of other states through cyberspace and from their operations centers. Considering the Internet's interconnectedness, these cyberattacks can also produce significant destruction (Giesen, 2013) which could even result in loss of life as a secondary effect.

Not only government organizations use cyberspace; the private sector, civilians, and academia employ the same resources that cyberspace provides such as the power grid. Therefore, cyberattacks can cause civilian entities to end up being collateral damage. The damage cyber weapons can cause these various organizations can be just as dangerous and costly as kinetic weapons. Consequently, when actors in cyberspace deploy cyber weapons, they should also bear the responsibility of support during the affected infrastructure's restoring and rebuilding phases. This transition phase is known as *jus post bellum* or justice after war. There needs to be planning for the aftermath of cyberattacks in addition to controlling proliferation of cyber weapons. This is especially important when state and non-state actors continue to deploy more sophisticated cyberattacks with no accountability, such as Stuxnet (2010) (Zetter, 2011), the cyberattacks against Estonia (2007), Georgia (2008) (Kaska, Talihärm, & Tikk, 2010), and South Korea (2013) (Sang-ho, 2014a). These attacks had no direct financial-gain intentions, but were intended to destroy or disrupt the selected targets, and were possibly conducted or at least sponsored by state actors.

1

A. CYBER WARFARE: JUS POST BELLUM FRAMEWORK DEVELOPMENT JUSTIFICATION

States enter into agreements and treaties to ensure adherence to established laws of war, aid the safety of their citizens, and provide humane treatment for their warfighters during armed conflict. As the international community develops new weapons, it also proposes and enters into new agreements such as those on the development and use of nuclear weapons. With the emergence of cyber weaponry and the risk cyberattacks pose to civilian populations, the international community needs to use the same international-agreement paradigm to control cyber-weapon development and ensure ethical conduct during and after cyberwars.

States are supposed to plan for jus post bellum activities when they enter into an armed conflict. However, even with adequate planning, states underestimate the scope of the post-conflict actions, which results in failed attempts to conduct proper post bellum activities. For example, the United States government expected a swift transition during the 2003 Iraq War, with a fast military departure after they established the new government; this was not the case and it showed the lack of consideration for post bellum activities (McCready, 2009). During an armed conflict, militaries' main objective is to win wars; therefore, they often misjudge stability operations and believe that, once the fighting concludes, the stability operations will be easy to accomplish. For instance, previous wars degraded Iraq's infrastructure; the 2003 Iraq War caused further destruction to food, water, security, and sanitation infrastructures, which considerably increased death rates (Burnham, Doocy, Dzeng, Lafta, & Roberts, 2006). This made post bellum actions harder to accomplish and greatly affected the ability to save lives and quickly reconstruct infrastructure. Orend (2007) believes that there is great uncertainty as to whether or not Iraq is better than it was before the 2003 war. This could be true since they are currently facing an occupation by the Islamic State of Iraq and the Levant (ISIL). ISIL took advantage of the void the United States and its coalition partners left before Iraq's full war recovery. If we cannot correct the situation with kinetic operations that have plethora of historical learning lessons, it will be even more difficult to get it right in cyberspace and to properly deal with the aftermath of cyberwars. There are still many uncertainties when releasing cyber weapons, and decision makers have limited understanding of the technology and ability to determine what the collateral damage will be.

Some weapons continue to cause harm many years after a war has ended. For example, minefields are still hurting local populations because they are either never removed or their locations are unknown (U.S. Department of State, 1994). States may need to deal with these types of issues for many years. The implications of releasing a computer virus have some similarities since a virus can continue to affect systems even after the conflict has ended, and it encounters many victims on its path that might not have the capabilities to respond. For instance, the Stuxnet worm, one of the most precise cyber-weapon released to date, targeted the Natanz facility (Zetter, 2011) and had direct collateral damage on many civilian machines as well as the indirect damage caused as a result of criminals using the source code to create virus variations for their own crimes (Lin, Allhoff, & Rowe, 2012). The damage might not equate to loss of human life; nonetheless, when a virus is involved, it affects many systems within seconds and may require millions of dollars to assess the damage and fix the problem. The cost depends on the number of affected systems, the labor hours required, and the required level of technical knowledge of those involved in the effort. A computer virus deployment thus raises ethical issues concerning state and non-state actors, whether attacks adhere to the laws of war, assessment of the cost to public and private organizations, and attribution.

States and the international community have established laws to deal with cyber crime, but what happens when these cyberattacks are not of a criminal nature? How do states and the international community deal with this emerging threat? The international community has not come to a consensus about what constitutes an act of war in cyberspace. They have given even less thought to what should happen after cyber conflict. This study analyzes International Humanitarian Law (IHL) and international treaties as they apply to after cyber conflict, explores current jus post bellum frameworks, analyzes the aid provided during the recovery period during two kinetic wars, and discusses the available international cyber organizations. All these concepts are used as a basis to design a cyber-warfare jus post bellum framework.

B.   THESIS PURPOSE

Vint Cerf stated in 2011, "the Internet is brittle and fragile and too easy to take down" (cited in Karlgaard, 2011). What he means is that any malicious actor with a connection to the Internet has the ability to cause harm in cyberspace. Many cyber systems such as industrial control systems are vulnerable because security was not a priority in the design process. One example is the Aurora vulnerability, which targets a sequence of electrical breakers to get them out of synchronization, which can make a system break down and cause physical damage; this vulnerability is still present today in many control systems (Zeller, 2011). States and non-state actors can target electrical systems from far away as the electric and other control systems continue to move their access to the Internet. States will continue to need cyber protection from aggressors and ensured justice.

The international community can seek to learn from previous examples and researchers' jus post bellum concepts to start the discussion on what a just peace looks like in dealing with cyber post-conflict. There are good examples of post bellum actions such as for World War II (WWII) where there was a positive outcome by fully considering post-conflict actions (McCready, 2009). The United States began post conflict planning during WWII almost at the beginning of the war and continued planning until the end of the war (McCredy, 2009). The U.S. used various entities to deal with post-conflict actions. Advance planning facilitated international cooperation to ensure proper actions for reconstruction and restoration and the establishment of a government. Some specialists, Orend (2007) and McCredy, advocate for states to pledge their jus post bellum activities and to make them an essential part of war planning. Then, the international community can hold states accountable if they fail to follow the promised post bellum actions. In the same way, the establishment of the proper cyber-warfare jus post bellum actions will help during post-conflict resolution. A cyber post-conflict framework before a major cyber conflict occurs will limit human suffering, and provide the steps for fast response, investigations, and accountability.

As the opening quote states, it is the responsibility of all states to ensure everlasting peace. Consequently, this study provides a framework for cyber post-warfare conduct, with emphasis on prevention and cyber weapons control. Additionally, the study examines the implications of deploying a cyber-weapon in terms of its reversibility, attribution, and planning of a cyber relief effort.

C.   THESIS OUTLINE

This thesis consists of seven chapters. Chapter I introduces the study's justification and the purpose. Chapter II defines IHL, current jus post bellum frameworks, and the treaties applicable to cyber jus post bellum. Chapter III surveys cyberattacks, attack vectors, cyberspace damage assessment, the effects of previously deployed cyberattacks on military, civilians, and private organizations, and the ability to contain and reverse them. Chapter IV discusses damage assessment for past kinetic operations, the organizations involved in the recovery effort, and available international cyber organization that can provide support during cyber conflicts. Chapter V analyzes responses to cyberattacks in a case study involving South Korea and North Korea. Chapter VI presents a cyber-warfare jus post bellum framework, proposes a cyberattack relief-effort flowchart, and offers a post cyberattack cost checklist. The thesis concludes with a summary and recommendations for future work.

THIS PAGE INTENTIONALLY LEFT BLANK

II.   BACKGROUND

War often leads to the dissolution of established governments and civil order, and the destruction of critical elements of a society's infrastructure, and this dissolution or destruction may result in the post bellum suffering or death of many in the defeated society. Victors have a moral obligation to ensure the security and stabilization of a defeated nation. Whenever practical and possible, they must provide the essentials of life (food, clothing, shelter, medicine, etc.) to those without them and repair or rebuild infrastructure essential to a vulnerable population's health and welfare. (Iasiello, 2004, p. 42)

A.   INTERNATIONAL HUMANITARIAN LAW

After Henry Dunant witnessed the bloodshed of the Battle of Solferino in 1859, he started the movement to establish the International Committee of the Red Cross (ICRC) to aid the wounded (Encyclopedia Britannica, 2013). Swiss citizens founded the ICRC in 1863, which later became the overseer of International Humanitarian Law (IHL), based on the Geneva and Hague Conventions (ICRC, 2002). The purpose of IHL is to provide suggested principles for states to enter into legal international contracts in the forms of treaties, declarations, or agreements which will provide protection during conflicts to civilians and personnel not participating in hostilities; it also restricts what weapons can be used (ICRC, 2002). However, not all states have ratified all the current IHL treaties and do not have to abide by the treaties they do not ratify; therefore the international community has customary international law, which binds all states (Henckaerts & Doswalk-Beck, 2005) to respect these customary international laws. As a result, the international community can find states in violation of customary law or established IHL treaties whether states are signatories of the treaties or not. Other international bodies involved in the preservation of international law are the United Nations (UN), the International Court of Justice (ICJ), and the International Criminal Court (ICC). These bodies and their responsibilities are depicted in Table 1.

Photo Removed Due to Copyright Restrictions

Table 1.   International Body Responsibilities
             (after ICRC, 2014; UN, 1945; ICC, 1998).

The UN is an international body created after World War II, which also requires states to abide by international law as part of its charter (UN, 1945). The General Assembly of the UN adopted resolutions to protect human rights during armed conflict and peace, to include establishing ad hoc courts to deal with human rights violations (Gasser, 1995). The Security Council is a branch of the UN that establishes steps to ensure or reinstate peace while ensuring human-rights protection (Gasser, 1995). The ICJ, which does not specifically address IHL, is the UN prosecution body to ensure states abide by international conventions and customary law (ICJ, 2015). The ICC is a judicial international body that specifically qualifies certain violations as war crimes (ICC, 1998). Essentially, states are supposed to abide by these customary laws during the conduct of armed conflict to avoid unnecessary suffering and to protect civilians, the wounded, prisoners of war (POWs), civilian infrastructure, and children; if not the international organizations can hold states and individuals accountable for war crimes (Henckaerts & Doswalk-Beck, 2005). States can use the ICJ and ICC to bring issues or IHL or customary international law violations against other states, individuals, or organizations and ensure war crimes are brought to justice (ICJ, 2015; ICC, 2014). The judges assigned to the ICC must have knowledge of criminal law, law procedures, IHL, and the law of human rights (ICC, 2014).

The ICRC, as the overseer of IHL, attempts to maintain IHL current with newly invented technology and warfare weapons to avoid unnecessary suffering. This was the case when the ICRC updated IHL to include treaties prohibiting the use of chemical weapons, including their "development, production, and stockpiling" (ICRC, 2002, p. 11). However, Dörmann (2001) argues that IHL is not weapon-dependent.

Currently there has been much discussion about how to translate IHL into the newly defined cyberspace domain. Harold Hongju Koh, a United States Department of State Legal Advisor, has said the U.S. government believes that the principles of international law apply to cyberspace (Koh, 2012). More recently, the *Tallinn Manual*, published by the North Atlantic Treaty Organization (NATO) Cooperative Cyber Defense Centre of Excellence, proposed that established customary international laws apply to cyber-warfare (Schmitt, 2013). Nevertheless, there are challenges to ensure an ethical cyberwar, such as possible collateral damage due to computer-system interconnectedness and the difficulty of attribution and damage assessment (Liaropolous, 2010). For example, one of those international rules is to distinguish between combatants and non-combatants in targeting, which raises questions due to links between civilian and military systems and the inability to contain a computer virus to a specific target.

Furthermore, the *Tallinn Manual*, IHL, and customary laws do not address the steps states should take after the conclusion of war or after states carry out a cyberattack, except for prosecution of war crimes violations (Schmitt, 2013; Henckaerts & Doswalk-Beck, 2005). Just as there are rules for the ethical consideration of the start (*jus ad bellum*) and conduct (*jus in bello*) of cyber armed conflict, we propose here that there should be rules for the ethical termination of a cyber armed conflict: jus post bellum—transition from war to peace.

B.   JUS POST BELLUM

IHL is guidelines for states to conduct righteous and ethical war. It attempts to ensure states remain within the legal framework during war, then referred to as just war. Just-war theory measures a state's right to go to war (jus ad bellum criteria) and states' conduct during war (jus in bello criteria) (Douglas, 2003). The jus ad bellum criteria are

9

just cause, right intention, right authority, reasonable hope of success, last resort, announcement of intention, and proportionality (Douglas, 2003). The jus in bello criteria are right intention, proportionality, and discrimination (Douglas, 2003). There has been much discussion of the frameworks of jus ad bellum and jus in bello. The international community must start to think about the ethical and moral actions states should take after a war has concluded. Since just-war theory or IHL does not provide a framework for justice after war, scholars advocate that jus post bellum is a critical pillar of just war and should not be ignored (Bass, 2004; Douglas, 2003; Orend, 2007; Österdahl, 2012; McCready, 2009). These theologists, scholars, and ethicists introduced a framework known as jus post bellum theory. This phase consists of the actions states take to ethically end wars and transition to peace.

Immanuel Kant is the first philosopher thought of as the founder of viewing warfare as consisting of three different pillars: "1. the right of going to war; 2. right during war; and 3. right after war" in his *Metaphysics of Morals* (cited in Stahn, 2006, p. 935). Kant also expressed in his *Toward Perpetual Peace*, as translated and publish by Yale University Press, that states involved in armed conflict should not conduct acts that will prohibit them from being able to reach peace (Kant, 2006). As an example, Kant (2006) believed that peace agreements that had ulterior motives should be invalid as is it not a peace agreement and it only postpones a new inevitable war. Additionally, Kant believed that a state's military superiority did not mean it could punish or force the defeated to recompense the victor (cited in Stahn, 2006).

Douglas (2003) believes just-war criteria are outdated and should be revisited for current times. Douglas contends that states go through a moral deliberation when starting and conducting a war and he advocates for the same moral deliberation during the termination of war, what he calls 'just result.' Douglas also believes that just-war theory has not provided adequate criteria for jus post bellum and this could result in more hostilities. Moreover, Douglas believes that humanitarian relief can limit war impacts and the possibility of new conflict.

Orend (2007) believes that jus post bellum has been mainly ignored due to tradition and because many just-war theorists include it as part of jus ad bellum. Orend

10

does concede that there should be a strong link between jus ad bellum and jus post bellum, but he also advocates for much more and therefore it should be a phase by itself of the just war framework, which should be based on Kant's concepts. Additionally, Orend advocates for a jus post bellum Geneva Convention that stipulates, "what the winners of war may and may not do to countries and regimes they have defeated" (p. 575). Orend proposes the following principles: rights vindication (human rights secured), proportionality and publicity (fair and public peace settlements), discrimination (distinction), punishment (hold aggressors accountable), compensation (possible mandated economic restitution), and rehabilitation (reconstruction). Essentially, he believes states should plan and have strategies for an ethical war transition. He stresses the benefits everyone will obtain with a set of established rules and measures, especially for difficult scenarios. He ascertains that these procedures will be worth it for the victors, defeated, and international community as a whole.

Bass (2004) believes that jus post bellum aids states to focus the war. Bass focuses on three central questions relevant to postwar behavior. The questions are:

> What obligations are there to restore the sovereignty of a conquered country and what limitations do these obligations impose on states' efforts to remake the governments of vanquished countries? What are the rights and obligations that belligerent states retain in the political reconstruction of a defeated power? Are these rights limited to the reconstruction of genocidal regimes, or can a case be made for the political remaking of less dangerous dictatorships? [And] What obligations might victorious states have to restore the economy and infrastructure of a defeated state? Conversely, do victorious states have a right to demand some kind of reparation payments from defeated states who were aggressors in the concluded war? (Bass, 2004, p. 385)

These are important questions to consider during post-war conduct to ensure a moral and ethical post war behavior and long lasting peace. Bass concluded that there are moral duties of victors when returning to peacetime; victors should exit immediately, unless it is a genocidal state in which case victors have a responsibility to aid in political reconstruction, and advocates for "prudence and proportionality" for reparations between victors and aggressors. Those moral duties might include not leaving immediately, as some states might require the victor to remain in place and aid in reconstruction of government entities and physical infrastructure.

Iasiello (2004) also agrees that the jus post bellum is undeveloped and its examination can save lives, especially in a time of assured and immediate victories. Iasiello proposes having a plan and vision for war termination, which will ensure actions to rebuilt, restore, and reestablish are not broken and abide by legal and moral guidelines. Iasiello introduces seven criteria for post-conflict standards of behavior: "a healing mind-set, just restoration, safeguards for the innocent, respect for the environment, post bellum justice, the transition of warriors, and the study of the lessons of war" (Iasiello, 2004, p. 40). All seven criteria are important for a peace-to-war transition. Additionally, Iasiello proposes a three-stage interrelated approach to just restoration to allow for healing: protectorship (protect and provide for the victor and defeated populace), partnership (victor and defeated work together to restore, rebuild, and repair), and ownership (establish self-governance and sovereignty). Just restoration highlights the importance of victors not leaving the defeated in a state of disarray and destruction. It is the victor and defeated responsibility to ensure cooperation to ensure an eventual return to normal or better.

Boon (2005), unlike the previous authors, believes that a link between jus ad bellum, jus in bello, and jus post bellum is not necessary. Boon advocates that the reason for war and how the war was fought should not affect the actions taken after war, which must still abide by justice principles. In addition, Boon highlights "the central tasks of post-conflict reconstruction: the establishment of law and order, preparation for free elections, establishment of the groundwork for independent institutions and the recognition of fundamental rights and liberties with the aim of eventual self-governance" (p. 290–291). To accomplish these task, Boon introduces three concepts: trusteeship (ethical and legal obligations to act in the best interest of the occupied state), accountability (hold people accountable for their actions), and proportionality (ability to assess the magnitude of legal intervention). Boon argues that a link is not necessary for ethical post-war conduct, especially for states that did not have the right to go to war or did not fight ethically: The international community should hold those states responsible for their unethical actions, but not excuse them from their responsibility in transitioning from peace to war ethically because they did not fight a just war.

Österdahl (2012) concludes that even though there is already law to ensure jus post bellum in combination with peace agreements, there is still a void within these laws to effectively establish peace after a war has concluded. Therefore, Österdahl believes that war-to-peace transitions require a jus post bellum methodology and transitioning tools. Österdahl also concludes there is a need for law specific to jus post bellum, but that governments might be against establishing it because of the complexity and the requirements to fulfill a transition from peace to war. Even though transitioning from war to peace can be a difficult task and event dependent, there are generalities that can be established to restore the peace.

Stahn (2008) believes that the international community has largely ignored the transition period from war-to-peace. Stahn agrees with Österdahl that current law is insufficient for jus post bellum, but also that it needs to be used to regulate the war-to-peace transition and not just as a moral slogan. Stahn argues that jus post bellum can essentially set rules and limitations for local and international actors. Stahn advocates for viewing jus post bellum as a whole by using established war-to-peace transition guidelines and their relationship. Stahn also states that due to the complexity of current wars, jus post bellum should also apply to "events other than classical wars," as well as be defined case-by-case because of the inability to have a clear understanding of the end of hostilities (pp. 333–334). Stahn does a good job highlighting that every war is different and the transition should be war-specific. The ability to develop additional guidelines for each war can expedite the transition.

James Turner Johnson argues that the aftermath actions are included and should be planned during the jus ad bellum phase (cited in McCready, 2009, p. 67). McCready (2009) disagrees with Johnson and argues that there needs to be a separate set of criteria to cover jus post bellum. He explains that jus post bellum is a misleading term as it is difficult to transition from war to peace due to major operations concluding and transition beginning before war is completely over. "The intent of establishing a jus post bellum category is to determine beforehand what these war-related responsibilities should be after the shooting stops and who should be responsible for them" (McCready, 2009, p. 68). McCready appeals for a set of guidelines that can ensure states are aware of their post-conflict responsibility before the end of the conflict.

Most scholars believe there is a need for an international establishment of jus post bellum criteria that will ensure that lasting peace is achieved post-conflict. Additionally, McCready, Orend (2007), and Iasiello (2004) agree that there should be a plan of action for post-war actions; Orend, Iasiello, and Boon (2005) advocate for ensuring accountability for unethical actions during conflict; Orend, Iasiello, and Bass (2004) stipulate some sort of compensation and or reconstruction aid post bellum; and Orend, Boon, and Kant (2006) recommend fair or proportionate aid and agreements. Wars are inevitable and after a war has ended, there could be widespread suffering and destruction; both victor and defeated have responsibilities to restore the state's essential services, transition to peace, and end suffering. Jus post bellum introduces frameworks to develop treaties that could address these problems.

C.   JUS POST BELLUM IN CYBERSPACE

Kant introduced jus post bellum framework in 1796 in the *Metaphysics of Morals* (Stahn, 2006). However, the international community views jus post bellum as an essential part of jus ad bellum and jus in bello (Anderson, 2014). It only gained more consideration in the 2000s, possibly due to the Iraq and Afghanistan wars. Since cyberspace is a new domain, much of the focus about cyberspace has been in the jus in bello and jus ad bellum as emphasized by the *Tallinn Manual* and the ICRC. Nonetheless, works by Giesen (2013), Denning and Strawser (2014), Rowe, Garfinkel, Beverly, and Yannakogeorgos (2011), and Liaropolous (2010), discussed below, can be used as a basis for analysis of cyberspace jus post bellum and the creation of a cyber jus post bellum framework.

Giesen (2013) agrees that customary law and the UN Charter are applicable to cyberwar for jus ad bellum and jus in bello, but not for jus post bellum. Giesen states that cyberspace is now a global common, the center of gravity, and societies are dependent on it, which means any threat against it can be debilitating. Therefore, Giesen advocates for a new international treaty for cyber jus post bellum implementation based on the Kantian jus post bellum. Giesen uses two criteria for an ethical cyberwar jus post bellum for the consequences of committing a war act, which consist of agreement violations that can disserve all people and conduct that makes peace impossible. She advocates an international agreement that bans any cyberwar act that will cause enough detrimental "economic and social damage" that peace will not be possible. She focuses on the prevention of cyberattacks rather than the actions after an attack was conducted or the war has ended, a deterrence approach to cyberwar such as with nuclear weapons.

Giesen's approach is similar to Geib and Lahmann (2012) who advocate for the protection of critical civilian cyber infrastructure. Article 56 of Additional Protocol I to Geneva Conventions of 12 August 1949 (API) (1977) outlines protected sites such as dams and dykes but also provides some stipulations that will allow a military force to target these. The international community could add critical cyber infrastructure to the protected sites list or an international agreement could be signed banning attacks on certain critical cyberspace targets. In addition, the repercussions of such cyber acts on such targets will need to be made sufficiently great to aggressors and guidelines for investigation and indicting infringers will need to be established.

Denning and Strawser (2014) advocate for cyber weapons use instead of kinetic weapons after the cyber weapon meets the jus ad bellum and jus in bello criteria. They argue that using cyber weapons can pose less risk to both friendly and adversary military and non-combatants. Denning and Strawser also argue that the use of cyber weapons can aid in the jus post bellum phase during stability and reconstruction. Their main argument in the reconstruction phase is that the lethality or permanent damage of cyber weapons is low. Therefore, the reconstruction phase will consist of restoring data from backup files, which will be faster than having to rebuild infrastructure after a physical attack. It might seem like Denning and Strawser are contradicting Giesen's proposed ban of cyber weapons. That is not the case, as the only time they are advocating for the use of cyber weapons in place of kinetic weapons will be dependent on the ability of the cyber weapons to have results that are more ethical.

Rowe et al. (2011) propose an international agreement similar to chemical weapons. The agreement would outline when states can use cyberattacks, it would require states to police cyber criminals, and it would stipulate which cyber weapons are acceptable. They argue that cyber arms control is possible now more than ever due to the increasing capabilities of forensic tools and the ability to observe cyberattack development. An acceptable weapons agreement would mandate the use of only attributable and reversible attacks and a state could use digital signatures with a cyberattack to establish attribution. An example of a reversible cryptography attack, as proposed by Rowe (2010), is "where the attacker encrypts data or programs to prevent their use, then decrypts them after hostilities have ceased." States will be encouraged to use reversible attacks if they are responsible for reparations on the attacked state and states understand that other cyberattacks can damage their reputation. Reversible attacks can also limit the escalation of force and satisfy the appropriate use of force. These revisable attacks will make it easier to restore systems to their original state. The biggest obstacle, they see is attribution due to states' not taking ownership of cyberattacks.

Liaropolous (2010) defines jus post bellum criteria based on the widely accepted Orend framework: Proportionality, Rights Vindication, Discrimination, Punishment, and Compensation. However, Liaropolous does not actually define how Orend's criteria apply to cyberspace. He argues that even though it might seem like waging war through cyberspace is more ethical and result in fewer casualties, it would not necessarily be the case. That is because a cyberattack can destroy public services such as electricity, transportation, and water, and possibly even paralyze a technical city, which will directly target critical infrastructure (Liaropolous, 2010). In addition, Liaropolous warns that due to the blurry escalation of force in cyberspace, the result can be a "bloody war" with more casualties that were supposed to be avoided. Therefore, Liaropolous advocates for the need of conventions to outlaw the development of cyber weapons that can be used as weapons of mass destructions.

All these scholars agree in the basic principles of creating some sort of cyber agreement for the use of cyber weapons and the outlawing of indiscriminate cyber weapons to stop cyber actors before they conduct a detrimental cyberattack. These agreements will focus on deterring cyber actors by having severe consequences for any violation. Additionally, critical infrastructure can be added to the protected sites and only cyber weapons proven to be more ethical should be used to limit human suffering and facilitate reconstruction post bellum.

D.   TREATIES AND ARTICLES APPLICABLE TO JUS POST BELLUM

As new atrocities occurred during war, the international community through the UN, ICRC, and other parties introduced new treaties, conventions, charters, and declarations to control armed conflicts and the subsequent peace. The basic principles of Law of Armed Conflict (LOAC) include distinction, proportionality, military necessity, and humanity (Carr, 2011). One important thing to note is that LOAC is often developed in response to incidents and to ensure they are not repeated. For example, in 1977, the ICRC added the API that includes further protection for civilians and civilian objects during warfare, but only 174 countries have ratified it (ICRC, 2014). This API specifies in Article 51 the protection for civilians from being military targets and Article 52 affords the same protection for civilian objects.

The UN charter (1945) does not specify anything about the LOAC as its main purpose is to maintain peace. Still, the UN passes resolutions to protect civilians, such as UN resolution 2675 in 1970. This resolution specifies that during "the conduct of military operations, every effort should be made to spare civilian populations from the ravages of war, and all necessary precautions should be taken to avoid injury, loss or damage to civilian populations" (UN, 1970).

As mentioned earlier, these international laws are mainly for jus ad bellum and jus in bello; nevertheless, some agreements do have post-conflict stipulations. The following treaties and charters extracted from the international law convey the range of stipulations about jus post bellum. For a more complete list of current international treaties, refer to Appendix A which lists current international treaties including the established date, number of state parties and signatories, main purpose, and the possible applicability to jus post bellum. ICRC (2014) is the source providing the following information for the listed international treaties, unless otherwise stated.

1. Hague Conventions

These conventions define the provisions for war declaration, belligerent conduct during war on land, the prohibition or restrictions of certain weapons and capturing in naval war, the conversion of merchant ships to warships, and the protection of hospital ships, neutral states, undefended locations, and cultural property. These conventions "embody customary international law"; as such, violators are to be prosecuted for war crimes after the termination of hostilities. After conflict, cultural property is to be returned, restitution made, and assistance provided for recovery after the conflict ends. In cyber-warfare, the establishment of neutral powers makes their territory impenetrable.

2. Geneva Convention

These conventions afford protection to the wounded, sick, medical units and personnel, chaplains, voluntary aid, civilians and personnel not taking part in hostilities, victims of international and non-international armed conflict, medical material and locations, shipwreck, and hospital ships. It also prohibits perfidy, provides guidelines for treatment of POWs, and facilitates the identification of protected personnel. Violations of these conventions are prosecutable under war crimes after the end of hostilities. Belligerents are to release and return POWs at the conclusion of the armed conflict. In cyber-warfare, the prohibition of perfidy can be an issue as many attacks can involve impersonation.

3. Conventions Prohibiting Certain Conventional Weapons

These conventions prohibit the use of weapons that cause excessive injury or have indiscriminate effects. Furthermore, additional protocols prohibit the use of weapons that produce undetectable fragments with x-ray and lasers causing permanent blindness, provide restrictions on the use of mines, booby-traps, incendiary weapons, and minimize "risks and effects of explosive remnants of war." Violations of these conventions are also prosecutable under war crimes after the end of hostilities. Additionally, states are responsible for marking, clearing, removing, or destroying "explosive remnants of war in affected territories" in attempts to protect people from additional harm.

4. Additional Treaties Prosecutable for War Crimes

The Declaration Concerning Asphyxiating Gases prohibits "the use of projectiles [that] the sole object…is the diffusion of asphyxiating or deleterious gases" and the Convention Statutory Limitations to War Crimes "established no statutory limitation for war crimes and crimes against humanity." Violations of these conventions are also prosecutable under war crimes after the end of hostilities.

5. Genocide

The declaration on the Prevention on the Convention and Punishment of Genocide establishes genocide as an international crime during peace and war. Violations of genocide are prosecutable under peace and war crimes.

6. Mercenaries

The Organization of African Unity Convention on Mercenaries provides guidelines to end mercenarism and calls for post-conflict prosecution and extradition. Furthermore, the Convention on Mercenaries makes the recruitment, use, financing, and training of mercenaries prosecutable.

7. Additional Rights Violations

The Convention on the Rights of the Child is aimed at protecting children and calls for the recovery and reintegration of children post-conflict.

8. UN Charter

The UN currently has 193 members (UN, 2014) bound by the UN Charter (1945) containing several articles that apply during jus post bellum or after an attack has been conducted. However, a state must first infringe the peace or commit an act of aggression. Therefore, through the UN General Assembly Resolution 3314 (1974), the UN defined an act of aggression and allows the UN Security Council freedom to determine if any particular act is considered an act of aggression.

a.   *Article 39*

Under this article, the UN Security Council bears response responsibility for "threats to peace, breaches of peace, and acts of aggression." The UN can use Article 41, which includes measures such as sanctions that do not involve armed forces, and or Article 42, which includes the use of an armed force, to respond to the armed attack. Even though what constitutes an act of aggression or armed attack in cyberspace is still being debated, this article is important due to the requirement of UN response after an attack has been conducted.

b.   *Article 51*

This article allows states to defend themselves against armed attacks and gives states the right to respond when under attack.

c.   *Article 92*

This article establishes the ICJ as the judicial body of the UN. The ICJ articles relevant to jus post bellum are discussed below.

d.   *Article 94*

This article stipulates that states will comply with the decisions taken by the ICJ. This means that after the ICJ has ruled on a case brought to it, the member states must abide by the decision.

9.   Statute of the ICJ

The UN Charter (1945) established the ICJ as the judicial body of the UN. Disputes and war crimes between states are brought to the court and under article 94, mentioned above, states are to comply with the court's verdict.

a.   *Article 36*

This article establishes the court's jurisdiction about "the interpretation of a treaty; any question of international law; the existence of any fact which, if established, would constitute a breach of an international obligation" (ICJ, 2015). In addition, the court decides "the nature or extent of the reparation to be made for the breach of an international obligation" (ICJ, 2015). This means that the ICJ has the power to apply law and issue verdicts.

b. Article 38

This article stipulates that the court will apply international conventions and customary law to matters submitted to it (ICJ, 2015). This article gives the ICJ leeway to determine if acts not explicitly outlined in resolutions or treaties are violations.

c. Article 41

This article gives the court the power to issue measures to protect states' rights (ICJ, 2015). That means that the ICJ can issue a mandate to protect states.

10. ICC

The Rome Statute established the ICC in 1998 and 154 states are parties to the ICC, but not the United States (ICRC, 2014). Unlike the ICJ that settles matters between states, the ICC settles disputes against individuals and organizations (ICC, 2014) and exercises authority over severe "crimes of international concern" (ICC, 1998). During jus post bellum, the ICC can settle violation disputes. Under Article 5, the ICC has jurisdiction over crimes of genocide, crimes against humanity, crimes committed during war, and acts of aggression. War crimes refer to violations of the Geneva conventions and international LOAC.

11. NATO

The North Atlantic Treaty (1949) is an international agreement and under Article 5 reserves the right of member states to respond in an individual or collective way to acts considered armed attacks. The response can include the use of an armed force and requires UN Security Council notification. The response is to cease once the UN Security Council has taken steps "to restore and maintain international peace and security." NATO is one example of an international organization that has agreements for collective response.

E.   CONCLUSION

In conclusion, the majority of IHL, international customary law, treaties, charters, and so on are concerned with the right of states to go to war and stipulations to fight wars ethically. The main consideration for the aftermath of war is the prosecution of war crimes and deterring actors with prohibition agreements and treaties. Nonetheless, these agreements can be used as an example to develop a new treaty for ethical cyber-warfare jus post bellum. For example, these international agreements already ban indiscriminate weapons before they are used, which would include indiscriminate cyber weapons, and mandate respect of neutral territories. In addition, the frameworks and ideas presented by the discussed theologists, scholars, and ethicists can aid in the creation of a cyber jus post bellum framework for an ethical transition from war to peace. A treaty outlining the jus post bellum criteria for cyber-warfare will be beneficial for the international community.

III. CYBERATTACKS

Policy makers need a basic understanding of the different types of cyberattacks: the feasibility of conducting cyberattacks through different vectors, their effects, ways of establishing attribution, and the ability to contain and reverse them. This will aid policy makers in generating correct policies and international agreements to deal with the aftermath of a cyberattack. In the same manner, an understanding of cyberattack characteristics and effects will help develop correct post-cyber-conflict actions.

News of cyberattacks is an everyday occurrence around the world. It is evident by news stories of cyberattacks to steal money, information, and intelligence, break computer systems, modify information, and or make information inaccessible to legitimate users. There is a huge cost associated with responding to cyberattacks on information systems, which includes assessing the damage, attempting to establish attribution, and restoring systems and information. For example, the Federal Bureau of Investigation (FBI) estimated that botnets have cost U.S. victims losses totaling 9 billion dollars (Demarest, 2014). Not all these attacks constitute an act of war; in fact, no single attack to date has been agreed by any consensus to be an act of war. These attacks have generally been categorized as criminal and have been costly. However, some of these cyberattacks were state-on-state and could have been considered an act of war. Cyberattack is a broad term because it encompasses low-level attacks and major attacks by any entity. Therefore, there should be a distinction between cyber act of war and other cyber activities. The distinction can be made in international agreements, with the understanding that to be categorized as a cyber act of war, the attack would have to meet a designated list of criteria. For example, Schmitt (2013) defines a cyber act of war by these criteria: severity, immediacy, directness, invasiveness, measurability of effects, military character, state involvement, and presumptive legitimacy.

Even though there should be a distinction between a cyber act of war and other cyber activities, aggressors in cyberspace use the same methods to develop and carry out cyberattacks. These actions usually include deciding on a target, establishing goals, conducting reconnaissance, deciding on the type of attack and attack vector, and carrying out the attack. Cyber criminals focus on financial gain and do not give too much thought to possible collateral damage. On the other hand, state actors should be more concerned with developing cyber weapons that can be contained or reversed and can achieve the same objectives, which would limit human suffering, collateral damage, and further public's acceptance and trust. Developers could check this through careful testing of the cyber weapon on target and non-target systems to ensure it has the desired effects. Cyber-weapon developers must be able to determine if the deployed weapon will meet the desired effects, and determine cascading effects, to inform the decision makers of cyber-weapon deployment consequences.

A.   TYPES OF CYBERATTACKS

States design cyber weapons to accomplish different effects depending on the desired outcome, unlike a kinetic weapon used mainly to destroy a target. The cyberattacks on computer systems affect confidentiality, integrity, and or availability. This section provides a description of various cyberattacks and their usage to achieve military objectives. It is important to note that technical expertise and financial backing are limiting factors for cyber-weapon development. However, there are cyberattacks readily available for a price that can cause damage without much technical knowledge, which enables non-state and developing states to use cyber weapons too. Paramilitaries and militaries can use publicly available cyberattacks, modify them, or apply their own developed malicious codes, to disrupt, destroy, deny, and degrade an enemy to obtain the military advantage.

Denial of service (DoS) and distributed-DoS (DDoS) are cyberattacks that target availability of computer systems to legitimate users. Aggressors would use one or multiple systems to swamp an Internet-connected system with data to render it or its resources unavailable (Schmitt, 2013). A military unit can use this attack to prevent communications or make air-defense systems unavailable during a military operation. According to Ponemon Institute (2013), DoS attacks are the most costly type of attack due to their frequency.

However, most attacks involve malware. Malware is malicious code that has negative effects on computer systems. Aggressors develop the code and deliver it through "attack vectors". Aggressors embed malicious code in software, firmware, and hardware; examples include logic bombs, rootkits, viruses, and worms (Schmitt, 2013). A military unit can use malware to destroy systems, delete data, or spy on their enemies. The Ponemon Institute (2013) reported an average of 49.8 days to resolve malware attacks, which equals an average cost of over 1.5 million dollars per incident.

An Advanced Persistent Threat (APT) consists of an aggressor that was able to gain access to a system and established a foothold into the system. APTs use various methods, as depicted in Figure 1, to break into computer systems while remaining undetected to gather intelligence or conduct other types of activities (Symantec, 1995). Military units can establish APTs to set up future sabotage activities.

Photo Removed Due to Copyright Restrictions

Figure 1.   Advanced Persistent Threat (from Symantec, 1995).

B.   CYBERATTACK VECTORS

Attack vectors are the method, people, or vessels by which cyber actors deliver cyberattacks. Aggressors decide on attack vectors in conjunction with the attack type and it can depend on the target's cyber-security posture. For example, an organization with out-of-date patches is an easier target for access exploits, as vulnerability lists and exploits to those vulnerabilities exists all over the Internet. Aggressors are able to determine devices' operating systems and versions during reconnaissance, which helps them determine the method of delivery. Attack vectors also facilitate targets of opportunity.

Social engineering often involves the use of deceptive emails, Webpages, and links that entice a target to unknowingly download malicious code. Social engineering includes phishing (mass emails), spear phishing (targeted emails), and whaling (executive-target emails). These attack vectors are commonly used because they are very successful with large groups of people (Kevin Mandia, Presentation, March 26, 2014). This means that at least one of the targets will click or download the malicious file, giving the attacker an access point into the targeted network. Social engineering can be the first step in either establishing an APT, logic bombs, or botnets.

Malicious insiders are personnel within an organization that are willing to aid an aggressor. Silowash, Cappelli, Moore, Trzeciak, Shimeall, and Flynn (2012) defined a malicious insider as someone who had or has legitimate access to information and deliberately performed acts that targeted the organization's confidentiality, integrity, or availability. Malicious insiders have the ability to cause more damage than other aggressors because they not only have access to the systems but they know more about the targeted system's vulnerabilities. Aggressors can recruit and use malicious insiders against air-gapped systems such as air-traffic control.

Botnets are networks of compromised computer systems directed by an aggressor to carry out coordinated cyberattacks (Schmitt, 2013). Computer systems in botnets are usually unwilling participants that augment the aggressor's ability to conduct cyberattacks. Aggressors use botnets to enhance DDoS attacks or as pivot points to hide their tracks.

Zero-day attacks refer to newly discovered vulnerabilities and are the most difficult attack vectors to develop and discover; they require higher technical knowledge because they involve finding an unknown system flaw or vulnerability to introduce the malicious code. The software vulnerabilities are unknown to software developers and vendors (Zetter, 2011) and hence they are hard to counter. Symantec reported that there is less than one zero-day exploit out of the one million malware samples they receive per month (Zetter, 2011), which demonstrates the rarity and difficulty of finding zero-day vulnerabilities.

Removable media, such as universal serial bus (USB) drives, could be used by a malicious insider or unwilling participant to inadvertently introduce malicious code if the removable media was not properly scanned before plugging it to the network. Other types of removable media that can transfer viruses include laptops, writable compact discs, and tablets. For example, Zetter reports that the attack vectors used to deliver the Stuxnet worm against Iran were an infected USB thumb drive and a malicious insider. Unknowing participants can also deliver malicious code through USBs, as in 2009 in the United Kingdom with the Conficker worm which resulted in over 15 million worldwide infected computer systems (Whittaker, 2013). Even after these incidents, Whittaker reports that U.S. Department of Defense continues to allow these devices on secure system to expedite work processes instead of security and policy adherence.

C. CYBERATTACK EFFECTS

This section will discuss three cases: Estonia (2007), Georgia (2008), and Iran (2010) to illustrate the different effects cyberattacks can have on systems, infrastructure, and civilians. In addition to these cases, the Sony Pictures Entertainment (SPE) hack will be discussed below and in a later chapter as these attacks are a good example of state-sponsored attacks. The effects can be physical, economical, and or social with excessive collateral damage. Even though no one has categorized these cyberattacks as armed attacks, the cases highlight the disregard for Law of Armed Conflict (LOAC) adherence seen in cyber-warfare-like attacks, especially in targeting civilian entities and infrastructure. In addition, states are legally and morally bound by LOAC whether they are taking part in hostilities or not.

In 2007, in response to relocating a Russian bronze-soldier war memorial, Estonia suffered cyberattacks for over a month (Kaska et al., 2010). The targets were government e-services Websites, banks, Internet infrastructure, and media outlets. Estonia's big Internet footprint and attack coordination made the attack more powerful and successful. Coordination of times, target lists, and instructions on how to carry out the attacks were made available to the public; therefore anyone with a connection that wanted to contribute could contribute. The attacks grew in intensity and sophistication, starting with ping requests, then later used malformed Web queries and botnets while hiding their identity though proxies and Internet Protocol (IP) address spoofing. Aggressors use proxies and IP spoofing to mask the attack origin. The botnets' command and control were placed in locations that would not cooperate with investigations, which highlighted the need for international agreements on cooperation, investigations, and prosecution of cybercrime and cyber-warfare. Between 95 and 97% of Estonians conduct online banking, so these cyberattacks damaged the Estonian economy because the ability for all businesses to function was stopped, even though total losses have not been reported. These attacks also had negative social effects since Estonia's primary means of communication between citizens and government is through the Internet. Even the information coming out of Estonia was severely restricted. Kaska et al. qualified these events as being in a higher category than cyber crime, yet Estonia only prosecuted one person for these attacks.

In 2008, Georgia was the target of cyberattacks coupled by kinetic Russian attacks (Kaska et al., 2010). Schmitt (2013) argues that since these cyberattacks were part of hostilities, LOAC should have governed them. Just as with Estonia, the targets included governments, news and media outlets, and financial organizations (Kaska et al., 2010). Making civilian organizations primary targets is the reason Schmitt argues that these attacks were in violation of LOAC. The attacks were coordinated and included botnets, DoS, DDoS, Web defacements, and e-mail spamming (Kaska et al., 2010). The DoS and Web defacement are easy to repair (Rowe, 2010), still these attacks were unethical because the Georgian Government was unable to communicate with its citizens (Kaska et al., 2010). This exemplifies another case where possibly a nation-state targeted civilian organizations and should be held accountable post-conflict for actions conducted during conflict.

In 2010, a Belarus security organization discovered the Stuxnet worm that had targeted the Natanz nuclear facility (Zetter, 2011). Symantec analysts believe the attack was to prevent Iran from building their nuclear weapon arsenal. The attack used malware against a Siemens industrial-control system and its vectors were zero-day vulnerabilities, a USB, and a malicious insider. The attack affected thousands of centrifuges and it was the first time that there was an observable physical reaction from a cyberattack. This cyberattack shows the secondary physical effects a cyberattack can have through code manipulation. Antivirus organizations updated and distributed prevention signatures, and even then, over 100,000 computer systems suffered collateral damage. Antivirus organizations can do as much as possible to prevent further computer infections, but some malware has the ability to evade those protections.

Because of the excessive damage cyberattacks can cause, cyber operations need to follow an operations-planning and targeting process to vet and validate legal targets and methods of attack. States would be in violation of LOAC if civilians are primary military targets without a strategic significance (Rowe, 2010), which has been the case with various cyberattacks. Cyber operators must be able to determine if the deployed weapon will meet the desired effects while taking in consideration LOAC limitations, such as prohibitions on indiscriminate weapons and on making civilians or protected objects primary targets.

D. CYBER-WEAPON DAMAGE ASSESSMENT

Conducting battle damage assessment (BDA) for conventional weapons is easier than conducting cyber-weapon deployment damage assessment. The three phases for conducting BDA are assessment of physical damage, functional damage, and functional assessment (DOD, 2013). More than one source may be required to accurately perform BDA, such as geospatial intelligence, video, and human intelligence, though sometimes one source may be sufficient (DOD, 2013). For example, after a kinetic weapon deployment, a flyover can reveal the physical damaged it caused and whether it achieved the objective. In cyberspace, it can be difficult to determine whether the damage is long lasting, as with viruses that can keep attacking until removed.

Determining damage in cyberspace includes assessing the value of the systems, the value of the data, the impact on the organization, and the difficulty of the restoration of the systems. Additionally, damage of cyberattacks can be direct, indirect, or derivative (Park, 2010). Park proposes an enumeration of costs to correctly assess the damage of a cyberattack, such as acquisition cost of the items or tools needed to recover systems, operations cost for both internal and external personnel, business-opportunity losses, and indirect cost such as reputation, weighted by the type of agency attacked. The Ponemon Institute (2013) report also identifies direct, indirect, and opportunity costs and adds to the list detection, investigation, containment, and information losses to determine the total cyberattack cost. Each portion of the assessments requires technical knowledge. The conduct of a cyberattack investigation can also take a significant amount of time because it requires digital forensics, which must be performed by experts if it is to be performed correctly and hold up in court (Casey, 2011). So there are several challenges if we are to properly conduct cyberattacks damage assessments.

As another perspective, damage assessment is described by Jakobson (2011) to include four steps to determine the impact of a cyberattack. He outlines the steps as attack point detection, direct impact assessment, impact propagation, and mission impact assessment (Figure 2). The steps are sequential. The objective of step 1 is to discover the target. There might be no damage and to find out if an attack was successful, it must meet certain conditions, such as a target having exploitable vulnerabilities. Step 2 consists of determining the impact on the affected system. Step 3 is to determine the impact to other systems the cyberattack touched. Step 4 consists of determining the impact from the combined steps in conjunction with the mission status. Jakobson's impact assessment can only be conducted in cyberspace if you have inside knowledge of how the cyberattack affected the enemy's mission. This lack of knowledge only allows for internal use of this impact assessment process.

Photo Removed Due to Copyright Restrictions

Figure 2.   Mission Cyber Security Assessment Process (from Jakobson, 2011).

Jakobson's assessment process does have difficulties with cyberattacks. For instance, belligerent and victim can easily observe a DDoS attack, but a belligerent may not be able to determine if a malware code is making a system malfunction as was intended. Proper damage assessment requires that the attacker have a way to continue receiving reports for what the deployed cyber-weapon is doing. If the victim takes the targeted systems offline, a common response to cyberattacks, it would be harder for the attacker to know if the cyberattack worked. Because of the difficulty of conducting BDA in cyberspace and inability to determine if the objective was achieved, a cyber unit may be encouraged to overkill with cyberattacks in the form of multiple simultaneous methods that can have extensive collateral damage and increase the difficulty of post bellum restoration of services.

E.   ATTRIBUTION

All the previously discussed attacks have had economic and social costs and no state has been held accountable; that should not be acceptable to the international community. For example, Schmitt (2013) claimed that the Stuxnet attack was discriminate as it only damaged the intended systems. This is untrue because no one took responsibility for the attack, hence the aggressor(s) did not have to deal with the cost to antivirus companies and the over 100,000 infected computers systems. Even when there has been no proved attribution for cyberattacks, efforts to attribute are not futile, as investigators can use some technical steps and other significant events to establish an acceptable level of attribution. In addition, nontechnical factors can provide enough attribution to incite international action.

Significant events such as political statements can establish some level of attribution. For instance, Russia was outspoken about their displeasure with Estonia's decision to relocate the bronze soldier and the cyberattack intensity was associated with other political events involving Russia (Kaska et al., 2010). These public actions encouraged the attackers to continue their efforts, and Russia should bear some responsibility. During the investigation of the Estonia attacks, Russia's government refused to cooperate or to take any action to stop the offenders (Clarke & Knake, 2010);

32

such lack of cooperation can suggest a culprit or at least an abettor. The degree of sophistication of the later attacks also suggests the Russian government most likely provided some type of aid.

Russia also most likely sponsored the 2008 Georgia cyberattacks, as it followed shortly afterward with kinetic attacks. Another example is the cyberattacks South Korea has endured over the years, which can be correlated to significant political or historical events for North Korea. That correlation and the lack of other obvious suspects makes North Korea the likely culprit. Other attribution indicators are the level of sophistication and whether the cyberattack lacked financial gain goals; as Zetter explains, Stuxnet had no financial gain and the level of sophistication pointed to a state cyber unit as its origin. However, a political or other significant event alone cannot be the sole determinant for state attribution since it is not hard for a state to fabricate evidence of involvement of another state.

Technical steps can establish attribution such as forensic analysis and tracking the attack origin. Nevertheless, finding the originating attack location can be misleading because, as Schmitt argues, it is easy to conceal the origin of an attack through IP address spoofing, botnets, or pivot point to hide their tracks. Rowe (2015) also discusses the inability to attribute attacks to nation-states even if we find the attack origin because it will be hard to establish that it was a state directed attack and not an individual acting alone. State cooperation to aid in the investigation and prosecution will help in such cases. Brenner (2007) argues that if the attack origin is from the same location over a length of time it can aid in establishing attribution. Additionally, Rowe (2015) suggests investigators conduct back tracing quickly enough before systems delete information to determine the true origin, which can be facilitated by unique packets or obtaining the systems involved. An analysis of the malware code can also establish attribution, since "the structure and style of the attack may inferentially identify the organization responsible for it" (Brenner, 2007, p. 408). Researchers, such as Krsul and Spafford (1996), have proposed the analysis of code characteristics to find code authorship, as programmers tend to reuse familiar language code and styles. Krsul and Spafford also ascertain that there are many other features within a program that indicate authorship such as blank lines, not just its structure. During Krsul's and Spafford's research, correct authorship was inferred even when skills improved and programmers changed some of their programming characteristics. Analyzing the malware to establish authorship by matching the attack to previous known malicious code or getting the actual systems involved in the attack can provide sufficient information for attribution through forensic analysis.

If the attackers conducted file exfiltration, an investigation may find the final location of the extracted files. The extracted files have a traversal path that may be trackable. Following the traversal path may introduce jurisdiction issues, as the packets may have traversed different states. However, if jurisdiction is not a problem, investigations can establish the origin of the traffic by a variety of means (Clark & Landau, 2010), and the final destination can also be established through the same process. The final destination "will necessitate a two-way exchange of information [which] requires the use of valid source addresses" (Clark & Landau, 2010, p. 38). Casey (2011) explains these extractions as having evidence linking offender and victim, similar to a physical crime scene reflected in Figure 3. He explains that an offender in the physical world might leave something behind that establishes a connection between victim and offender, and in the same way a cyber actor can leave traces behind such as logs or extracted files. Essentially, "there will always be evidence of the interaction, although in some cases it may not be detected easily" (Casey, 2011, p. 16).

Photo Removed Due to Copyright Restrictions

Figure 3.   Evidence Transfer Physical and Digital Dimensions (from Casey, 2011).

The 2014 SPE hack was attributed to North Korea (FBI, 2014). SPE and movie theaters were threatened to stop movie distribution (FBI, 2014) of a satirical movie with the plot to murder the North Korean leader (FoxNews.com, 2015). Clearly, North Korea was unhappy with such a movie and was the major suspect in the cyberattacks. The FBI also used technical steps to establish authorship by correlating previously used malware linked to North Korea in signatures and algorithms. In addition, the FBI recognized in the attacks some IP addresses previously used for attacks that had been associated to North Korean cyber actors. Additionally, the attacker used the same tools in March 2013 attacks against South Korea, which the FBI attributed to North Korea (FBI, 2014). This particular cyberattack was a clear violation of international and customary established laws, as the primary target was a civilian organization targeted by a nation-state. However, it would not be enough for the FBI to say who did it for worldwide acceptance without tangible proof. This is because others counter the claim that this particular attack was by North Korea (FoxNews.com, 2015). Nonetheless, this case sets precedence for attributing a particular attack to a nation-state.

F.   CONTAINABILITY AND REVERSIBILITY OF CYBER WEAPONS

Containment of cyberattacks is an important issue in repairing the damage of such attacks. For instance, once a worm malware attack commences, it may take only seconds for the worm to propagate and infect hundreds or thousands of computer systems. In the case of Stuxnet, the aggressors designed the attack to target explicit software and hardware combinations (Schmitt, 2013). Even though it targeted a closed network, it still managed to infect civilian computer systems. The LOAC does allow for collateral damage necessary to achieve a significant military objective, so long as the attacker seeks to minimize collateral damage and believes it is not excessive, and damage is easier to determine with kinetic attacks due to their deterministic nature. Conversely, the concealment that cyberspace provides to aggressors makes them more likely to deploy cyberattacks and to be careless during those attacks. This is especially true with the difficulties of attribution and ease of plausible deniability in cyberspace. Some cyberattacks are uncontainable because that is their nature, such as self-replicating worms and viruses. Nevertheless, other cyberattacks can be precise, such as specifically crafted

35

malware, DoS, DDoS, and APTs. Despite the longer time to design and test a precise cyber-weapon, it is a states' responsibility to ensure minimal collateral damage and to abide by the LOAC.

One way to reduce long-term collateral damage is for states to design cyber weapons to be reversible as suggested by Rowe (2010). Rowe proposes four different reversible attacks: cryptographic attacks (encrypting a victim's information), obfuscating attacks (reorganizing data or software), withholding-information attacks (making data unavailable), and resource-deception attacks (creating deceptive messages). The reversibility that these attacks provide allows the aggressor to undo the damage quickly, as for example providing the decryption key for encrypted data (Rowe, 2010). This could be useful because most attacks require a significant amount of resources to reverse. It might be difficult to find the attack (Rowe, 2010), especially for attacks such as APTs, and the cost of an attack rises as the time to resolve it increases (PI, 2013). In addition, as the level of knowledge required increases to reverse the attack, the costlier it gets. Damage to data may be reversible but still costly, especially concerning physical and psychological effects (Rowe, 2010). Reversing effects can be costly because the attack has to be found, and the organization would have to conduct a damage assessment and forensic analysis, restore systems and data from backups, update antivirus software, and notify victims if data was stolen. Furthermore, victims would never be able to recover additional losses from non-availability or loss of intellectual property, especially without attribution.

G.   CONCLUSION

The deployment and proliferation of cyber weapons will continue to grow. Geers, Kindlund, Moran, and Rachwald (2013) claim that we will continue to see an increase in nation-state cyber-weapons usage, mainly because of the lack of attribution. States can use various types of cyberattacks and methods of delivery in cyberspace. These attacks can have significant psychological and physical effects. These cyberattacks are costly and establishing attribution to a nation-state can aid during conflict resolution, clean up, and restitution (Rowe, 2015).

It will be important to recognize cyberattacks that are part of cyberwar, then assign state attribution. An aggregation of technical and significant factors can facilitate attribution. Clark and Landau (2010) proposed that when nation-states conduct data exfiltration the attribution level does not have to meet the same requirements to stand up in court, as it becomes a national security issue. In addition, Casey (2011) proposed having a set of standard procedures for the collection of evidence after an attack. The international community can facilitate this by establishing cooperation agreements where a neutral third party would handle international investigations. This organization would be essential for the international community to establish attribution and ensure accountability. Cooperation on investigations and prosecution is easier said than done, as there are states that will not cooperate because they mandated or encouraged the attack, or because the state might benefit from the cyberattacks and be willing to turn a blind eye. This is where established international bodies and national policy are helpful for such things as sanctions. For example, the United States has issued sanctions in retaliation to North Korea's SPE hack (FoxNews.com, 2015), which shows to the world the U.S. government's certainty of their culpability. The international community can also use attribution and accountability as deterrents because they can set precedents for states violating customary and established international laws.

THIS PAGE INTENTIONALLY LEFT BLANK

IV.   PAST KINETIC OPERATIONS

When required to achieve national strategic objectives or protect national interests, the U.S. national leadership may decide to conduct a major operation or campaign involving large-scale combat, placing the United States in a wartime state. In such cases, the general goal is to prevail against the enemy as quickly as possible, conclude hostilities, and establish conditions favorable to the [Host Nation], the United States, and its multinational partners. Establishing these conditions often requires joint forces to conduct stability operations to restore security, provide essential services and humanitarian relief, and conduct emergency reconstruction. (DOD, 2011a, p. V-31)

A.   STABILITY OPERATIONS

Some of the authors urge for a jus post bellum plan before the start or cessation of hostilities to ensure an easier war to peace transition during a conflict (Orend, 2007; Iasiello 2004; McCready 2009). The U.S. military does follow this advice by preparing plans for jus post bellum activities during the operation-planning process. The military-planning manuals refer to these as stability operations. Understanding stability operations and analyzing past operations post-conflict activities can help to frame cyber conflict activities. This section will focus on the 2003 Iraq War and the 1998 Kosovo War actions during the operations' reconstruction phase, the entities involved during the relief effort, reconstruction cost, recovery challenges, and possible cyber considerations to extrapolate cyber conflict similarities and differences.

Stability operations are generally defined as actions to secure and restore essential services following any type of operation (DOD, 2011a). The operation-planning process consists of six phases as depicted in Figure 4: shape, deter, seize initiative, dominate, stabilize, and enable civil authority. Transitions between phases mark a clear distinction in objectives; each phase requires planning and preparation; each phase sets provisions and conditions for the next phase; and phases can be interconnected. For example, minimizing collateral damage when conducting combat operations in the dominate phase facilitates stability operations during the stabilize phase.

Photo Removed Due to Copyright Restrictions

Figure 4.   Phasing Military Operations (from DOD, 2011a, p. V-6).

Stability activities will be the stabilize-phase main objective with combat operations taking a smaller role (DOD, 2011a). "The intent in this phase is to help restore local political, economic, and infrastructure stability" (DOD, 2011a, p. V-9). Civil-military operations are important during this period, and they are intended to secure the population and key infrastructure, rebuild, and restore public services (DOD, 2011a). Stability-operation activities include providing limited local government and humanitarian relief, rebuilding government and institutions infrastructure, restoring essential services, supporting economic growth (DOD, 2011a), making peace agreements, and restoring, upgrading, and modernizing communication systems and infrastructure (DOD, 2011b). In many modern states, these essential services can include rebuilding or restoring cyber infrastructure as many states provide medical and government services through cyberspace. Economic growth is also reliant on cyberspace. Consequently, states must assess the damage to be able conduct the appropriate activities during stability operations.

B.   DAMAGE ASSESSMENT KINETIC VERSUS CYBER

Damage assessment is a fundamental task of jus post bellum. During an attack states are supposed to abide by proportionality to minimize collateral damage and even use non-lethal means, if possible, to achieve the desired results and minimize activities during stability operations (DOD, 2011b). However, during a conflict, damage to infrastructure is inevitable, and states and the international community must assess these damages. Since kinetic attacks cause some sort of physical damage, kinetic operations facilitate damage assessments due to easily observable effects. A kinetic attack is also somewhat deterministic, as the kinetic weapon will have a range of destruction. In contrast, the damage caused by a cyberattack is more difficult to assess, in determining the number of affected systems, the affected data value, and the effects on untested systems and society. There can also be unknown effects for kinetic and cyber weapons, such as negative political effects depending on the collateral damage. Still, cyber weapons can provide a non-lethal means to achieve the same effect and minimize stability operations.

After the 2003 Iraq War cessation of initial hostilities, Britain and the United States expected a 25 to 100 billion dollars cost in reconstruction (Schmickle & Writer, 2003). The cost would include reconstructing or restoring harbors, railroads, water system, electricity, agriculture, and medical services. The immediate efforts would include clearing mines from railroads and providing food and medical service to the local population. The issues faced by coalition forces and other involved entities are the years of infrastructure deterioration prior to the conflict, competing priorities of what is to be fixed first, and population impatience over the slow reconstruction process (Schmickle & Writer, 2003). The actual cost in Iraq was considerably higher due to the prolonged reconstruction process.

After the 1998 Kosovo War, the United Nations (UN) survey concluded that there was significant damage, mostly due to the fleeing Serbian forces' looting (Kifner, 1999). The damage included destruction to two-thirds of housing, schools, health facilities, agriculture, and water pollution. The World Bank survey team reported the damage to be three to four billion dollars, less than originally expected, to fix minor loss of electricity

41

and infrastructure (Daily Commercial News, 1999). The difficulties of assessing the damages were the conflicting damage assessments outcomes and the time it would take to accurately assess the damage. Furthermore, there was a lack of coordination between aiding organizations, which resulted in duplicate efforts (Dursun-Ozkanca, 2009).

During the Kosovo War, the U.S. military discussed using a cyberattack. They decided against using cyber weapons on the enemy's air defense systems and civilian services in Yugoslavia due to effects uncertainty and issues with abiding by the Law of Armed Conflict (Graham, 1999). Likewise, at the beginning of the Iraq War, cyberattacks were cancelled due to possible collateral damage (Elliott, 2010). Even though John Arquilla confirms there was some use of cyber to deceive Serbian air defense systems during the Kosovo War (cited in Elliot, 2010), the limited use of cyber weapons highlights the insecurities of using cyber weapons. These decisions also demonstrate that the military was already taking into account the consequences of carrying out cyberattacks twenty years ago, and calls attention to the challenges cyber operators will be facing when assessing cyber weapons risks.

1.   **Jus Post Bellum Cost**

As of December 8, 2014, the U.S. Congress has appropriated a total of 815 billion dollars for the Iraq War cost and requested 5 billion dollars for Fiscal Year (FY) 2015; Congress continues to request funds to facilitate Iraq's ability to counter terrorist groups, as it has not fully transitioned to a peaceful state (Belasco, 2014). These costs include for example reconstruction efforts, foreign aid, and the training of Iraqi security forces. As Figure 4 shows, all operation phases included planning and actions for stability activities, with stability operations taking a bigger role as the operation progresses. Therefore, even when hostilities have not completely ended, there are activities including jus post bellum actions conducted in an effort to transition to a peaceful state. Table 2 is a depiction of the activities and amounts spent over the past 12 years and expected cost for FY2015 to transition power to the Iraqi people. The actual cost in Iraq was underestimated because a swift transition was expected instead of the prolonged reconstruction process. The Iraq War also demonstrated the United States and coalition forces' commitment to assist a state even after major combat operations were complete and forces withdrawn. This aid is in part because terrorists and failed states pose a threat to the international community.

Photo Removed Due to Copyright Restrictions

Table 2.   Iraq War Operation Cost (after Belasco, 2014).

The United States total cost of support efforts for the Kosovo War was approximately 6.2 billion dollars; this cost included humanitarian aid, reconstruction support, and military operations (Ek, 2000). As a North Atlantic Treaty Organization (NATO) led operation, the majority of reconstruction cost was to be the European Nations' responsibility (Ek, 2000). The United States and allied nations' war cost and activities are portrayed in Table 3. The amounts are those either state provided or pledged and reported to the Congressional Research Services (CRS). Therefore, the total presented here is an estimate as some states either did not report all assistance value or contributed through other channels not listed in the CRS report. The total amount for the Kosovo war cost was approximately 11.8 billion dollars. It is important to understand that during the Kosovo War there was a clear demarcation on the transition from offensive operations to stability operations, which was different from the Iraq War. In addition, the Kosovo War emphasized the collective effort required to assist a state's transition to peace, even if they were not the aggressors or warring parties.

Photo Removed Due to Copyright Restrictions

Table 3.   Kosovo War Cost (after Ek, 2000).

The Ponemon Institute 2013 Research Report estimated cyberattacks to cost an average of 32,469 dollars per day and require an average of 32 days to address. This equates to a cost of over one million dollars per cyberattack. The reference to a cyberattack in this report is to criminal activity. However, the cost and response actions might be similar when responding to a cyberattack on, say critical infrastructure. Moreover, state and non-state actors can use these same criminal cyberattacks as offensive warfare weapons. The cost will be different depending on various factors, i.e. the time it takes to respond to the attack, the organization size, and the type of attack, with organizations experiencing higher malicious code attacks and denial of service being the costliest (PI, 2013). The response actions, depicted in Figure 5, include internal actions such as detection, recovery, containment, and investigations and external costs, such as equipment damage and revenue loss (PI, 2013). This framework can help an organization to determine the internal and external cyberattack cost. Additionally, cyber defensive actions can minimize the cost of an attack, such as deploying security intelligence systems (PI, 2013).

Photo Removed Due to Copyright Restrictions

Figure 5.   Cost Framework for Cyber Crime (from PI, 2013).

A straight cost comparison between the Iraq and Kosovo Wars versus a cyberattack cannot provide an accurate estimate of cost savings due to the cause and effects of a kinetic attack versus a cyberattack. But the comparison can encourage the use of a tested ethical cyber weapon that can have the intended effects instead of a kinetic attack that can cause more destruction and possible loss of life. However, cyberattacks require further considerations, such as that various cyberattacks already out in the wild can be manipulated and used against any target, states are developing cyberattacks that can have more detrimental effects, and a state can paralyze a technological state without even stepping foot on the attacked state. As an example, as more industrial systems increase their target area by connecting to the Internet, states will be able to target these systems without having physical access to the facilities, which can result in loss of life effects. Therefore, the international community should seek to protect populations and attempt to control cyber weapons.

2. Entities Involved in Reconstructions

Many entities are involved during transitions from war-to-peace. These organizations aim to end suffering and aid states to recover and flourish after an armed conflict. "No single actor can meet the challenges of peace-building and reconstruction by itself. Cooperation and coherence are key factors in successful international peace-building operations" (Dursun-Ozkanca, 2009, p. 31). The number of entities involved points to the necessity of having a collective effort to ensure success during jus post bellum.

a. 2003 Iraq War

In addition to providing UN resolutions after a conflict, the UN agencies involved before the Iraq War and continuing to help the Iraqi people were:

- The Office of the Iraq Programme Oil-for-Food, which helped a sanctioned Iraq sell oil to meet Iraqi humanitarian needs (Coipuram, 2003).
- The Mine Action Programme for Northern Iraq, which finds and clears mines, educates the population, and rehabilitates victims (Coipuram, 2003).

- The UN Children's Fund, which protects children during the war (Coipuram, 2013).
- The UN Development Programme, which battles poverty (Coipuram, 2003).
- The World Food Programme, which battles hunger (Coipuram, 2003).
- The World Health Organization, which provides health assistance (Coipuram, 2013).
- The UN Environment Program, which provides education and environmental recovery (Coipuram, 2003).
- The UN High Commissioner for Refugees, which protects refugees (Coipuram, 2003).
- The UN Food and Agriculture Organization, which identifies machinery needs and provides fuel and assistance to begin agriculture (Schmickle & Writer, 2003).

The U.S. agencies that supported or continued to assist Iraq's post-conflict recovery were:

- The U.S. Agency for International Development and Office of Reconstruction and Humanitarian Assistance for reconstruction efforts (Schmickle & Writer, 2003).
- The Office of Foreign Disaster Assistance for humanitarian and reconstruction assistance (Schmickle & Writer, 2003).
- The U.S. Navy Engineers for harbor repair (Schmickle & Writer, 2003).

Other nongovernmental organizations involved in Iraq include:

- The International Committee of the Red Cross, which protects war victims (Coipuram, 2003).
- The Human Rights Watch, which protects human rights (Coipuram, 2003).
- The Oxfam International, which battles injustice, poverty, and misery (Coipuram, 2003).

These lists do not include other states and coalition partners that helped in the reconstruction efforts and provided humanitarian assistance, such as Spain, Britain, and Kuwait (Schmickle & Writer, 2003).

b. *1998 Kosovo War*

In addition to the states listed in Table 3 that provided humanitarian aid, refugee assistance, and military and peacekeeping operations support, the World Bank and the UN helped to conduct Kosovars needs surveys, such as assessing destroyed homes and infrastructure, medical needs, and electricity requirements (Daily Commercial News,

1999). During or after the Kosovo War, the UN Interim Administration Mission in Kosovo was in charge of setting up an interim government; the UN High Commission for Refugees Agency provided humanitarian assistance; the Organization for Security and Co-operation in Europe was to provide "democratization and institution-building", the European Union (EU) was to aid in reconstruction and economic development; and NATO would provide "military protection" (Dursun-Ozkanca, 2009). All these organization were trying to help Kosovo establish enduring peace.

C. INTERNATIONAL CYBER ORGANIZATIONS

International coordinated efforts can make a transition from conflict-to-peace easier. There are already established international organizations that can aid states during a cyber conflict, which benefits cyberspace. These international organizations include the Computer Emergency Response Teams (CERTs), the Forum of Incident Response and Security Teams (FIRST), the Cooperative Cyber Defense Centre of Excellence (CCDCOE), the International Telecommunications Union (ITU), the World Summit on the Information Society (WSIS), the Organization for Economic Co-operation and Development (OECD), the European Network and Information Security Agency (ENISA), and the International Multilateral Partnership against Cyber Threats (IMPACT) and have the following responsibilities (Ferwerda, Choucri, & Madnick, 2010).

CERTs: These cyber centers' principal charter is to ensure network availability. They do it through responding to emergencies and advancing security tools. Currently there are 200 centers with various levels of expertise and structure. These centers began as non-profit organizations, but many are public-private trusts. Essentially, they find and report cyber vulnerabilities, advance a holistic threat understanding, respond to threats, and encourage communication between security vendors, users, and private organizations.

FIRST: This body advances information sharing between security organizations and incorporates CERTs at various levels.

CCDDOE: This NATO cyber organization is responsible for educating, training, and responding to cyberattacks against NATO members. Although not all NATO members are part of CCDDOE, it can support less technologically advanced members to deal with cyberattacks.

ITU: This is an international body that enhances understanding of legislation, botnets, and CERTS, provides tools for organizations to conduct self-assessments and threat response, promotes cyber education, and promotes cyber security cooperation.

WSIS and OECD: These world conferences on cyber security bridge the gap between various parties, such as academia, government, and security professionals and promote information sharing. OECD also publishes conference papers, guidelines, and best practices.

ENISA: The EU established this body to improve their ability to deal with and respond to cyber issues. ENISA focuses on cyber education, promoting best practices, and works with regional CERTs.

IMPACT: This is an ITU-sponsored international body. IMPACT responds to threats, conducts data analytics, maintains a research center, and provides real-time warnings to UN member states and defense resources.

Photo Removed Due to Copyright Restrictions

Figure 6.   Key Intergovernmental Institutions (from Ferwerda et al., 2010).

In developed states such as the United States. there are national cyber organizations. However, even the White House feels that the government is not structured to respond to the increasing cyber threats (cited in Ferwerda et al., 2010). Even though cooperation between these organizations has been increasing, they also believe it is not sufficient. The relationships between the different cyber organizations are shown in Figure 6, and also highlights that there is still more work to do on ensuring links are established between the organizations. The international community can benefit from open communication between all these organizations and collective cyber response because states will be better prepared for future cyberattacks, will have a holistic understanding of the threat, will further cyber education; and can establish solutions for known cyberattacks.

D.   CONCLUSION

The following observations can be made of the differences between kinetic and cyber conflict.

Observation 1: It can be difficult to correctly assess damages for kinetic and cyberattacks if many entities are involved. Still, the ability to observe a kinetic attack's physical effects makes it easier to determine the damage. For a cyberattack, for instance, a deployed computer virus can continue to infect systems even after the cessation of hostilities similar to landmines that continue to claim innocent victims and prevent reconstruction efforts post-conflict (U.S. Department of State, 1994). There are agreements regarding the use of mines because of their indiscriminate nature and lingering effects (ICRC, 2014); analogous agreements are lacking for cyberspace. In addition, the cyber reconstruction effort might not even need personnel in the affected state, if say reversible attacks are used.

Observation 2: Kinetic attacks have effects that may not be feasible with a cyber-weapon. Therefore, states cannot substitute one for the other. Even so, the greater a state's Internet footprint, the greater an adversary's ability to paralyze that state. For example, in Estonia, there are over 150 e-public services, 95% of Estonians do online banking, and 98% of Estonians have Internet access (Kaska et al., 2010). This big

Internet footprint allowed attackers in 2007 to cause more economic damage than was possible in a poorly networked country.

Observation 3: Kinetic attack attribution is usually not an issue because the warring parties are known. By contrast, attribution becomes a difficult, albeit not impossible, task in cyberspace due to plausible deniability. States and organizations can establish some type of cyberattack attribution through forensic analysis and intelligence gathering. Nevertheless, the international community can make attribution easier through agreements and investigations.

Observation 4: In the same way that defeated states or states facing internal turmoil need international aid to recover after the conflict, states lacking the technical ability to respond to major cyberattacks will need international help due to the level of expertise required to respond to cyberattacks. The established international, regional, and national cyber centers are helping to bridge this gap, but more cooperation is needed between these bodies.

Observation 5: A long list of established organizations support states during the aftermath of kinetic wars, whereas cyber organizations that provide assistance in the fight against malicious cyber actors are few and still developing.

Observation 6: Cost alone cannot be the determinant to use a kinetic attack over a cyberattack and vice versa, as there are other factors to consider such as desired effects and weapon ethicality.

Post-conflict activities are important if the international community seeks to establish long-lasting peace. Actors cannot plan for everything, but having transition and exit plans before conducting stability actions can make the transition smoother. Victors and defeated are integral part of the recovery and reconstruction effort regardless of who was the aggressor. If international organizations do not get involved, they may be enabling perpetual conflict, as some states do not have the capabilities to recover from a war. For example, the international community came together to help during the Kosovo and Iraq recovery periods, though most did not contribute to the destruction. In addition, a collective effort is more effective as demonstrated by the international effort in the two wars. The cooperation will require open lines of communication and a coordinated effort to limit duplicate efforts (Dursun-Ozkanca, 2009), which will aid in setting priorities, understanding the population's needs, and ensuring a successful recovery.

V. CASE STUDY: NORTH KOREAN CYBERATTACKS

As a minimal requirement, victors must return to the fields of battle and help remove the instruments of war. As a maximal requirement, victors must assist in the repair of the social infrastructure. Proscribed by such a principle would be of the vanquished and disregard of the fact that, for many innocent victims, the war continues after surrender. (Schuck, 1994, p. 982).

A. INTRODUCTION

Accessing or breaking into systems with a malicious intent violates established computer laws, such as the U.S. Computer Fraud and Abuse Act. Locating and stopping international computer crime continues to improve with the Council of Europe Cybercrime Treaty, although only 42 states have ratified it (CoE, 2014). Additionally, state governments can be involved in similar or more devastating attacks against another state's public or private sector, what we refer to as cyber-warfare. This raises ethical and moral issues on the proper procedures when dealing with government-sponsored cyberattacks after the fact, mainly adherence to International Humanitarian Law (IHL), customary international law, jus post bellum theory, the cost associated with restoration and dealing with these types of attacks, and the possible inability to contain the cyberattacks to only military objectives.

It is helpful to examine a case study. In the context of state-on-state cyberattacks, this case study's objective is to place into perspective the actions the attacked state and the international community can take during the aftermath of a state-sponsored cyberattack. Proper actions during the aftermath of a cyberattack are important to ensure aggressors abide by just-war theory, IHL, to maintain the peace and allow for just reparations. This case study will include steps taken after the attack and considerations for the start of investigations, possible emergency response organization actions, cost associated with the attacks, assignment of state responsibility, and use of international organizations intervention to settle the dispute. In view of the few cyber-warfare-specific laws, customary international law can apply to cyberspace, especially to the increased possibility of collateral damage in cyberspace. The assumption should be that cyberattacks are "subject to IHL just as any new weapon or delivery system has been so far when used in an armed conflict" (Dörmann, 2001). Moreover, the Additional Protocol I to Geneva Conventions of 12 August 1949 (1977), Article 36, stresses the responsibility of states to ensure any new weapon deployment abides by international law. Therefore, the international community needs to hold state governments accountable for the destruction due to cyber operations by supporting victim states during the conduct of investigations, establishing attribution, and enforcing international laws.

B. NORTH KOREA

Relatively little is known about Democratic People's Republic of Korea's (DPRK) intentions. Nevertheless, one of the recognized goals of North Korea is to continue pursuing the union of the Koreas while maintaining control (Maxwell, 2013). The alliance of the United States and Republic of Korea (ROK) is standing in the way of this goal; therefore, severing the United States and ROK alliance is important to the DPRK to allow for reunification (Maxwell, 2013). The ROK reported that from 1953 to 2011, the DPRK violated the armistice 221 times, conducted 26 military attacks, and continues escalating their actions (Hae-in, 2011). These physical actions could be an attempt to continue attacking the United States and ROK alliance, and to demonstrate to the ROK that they still have the power and resolution to cause damage. If the United States removed ROK support, the DPRK will have a greater likelihood of winning during an altercation with the ROK and re-unifying the Koreas.

The small amount of information from DPRK may be because North Korea highly controls the information that comes out to the world; they even designed their own intranet and operating system (OS) to contain the information their citizens can access and that circulates out of their borders. The DPRK government restricts access to information and websites through their home-built intranet and "Red Star" OS, which is mostly available for government, universities, and government-run institutions (Ventre, 2011). According to the Asia Pacific Network Information Centre (2014), DPRK has been assigned the Internet Protocol (IP) range 175.45.176.0 - 175.45.179.255 and Autonomous System (AS) 131279 managed by Star Joint Venture Internet Service

Provider Company. According to Robtext.com, AS 131279 is directly connected to China's AS 4837. DPRK uses Chinese servers to host and broadcast information and only a few identified personnel have access to the Internet (Ventre, 2011). North Korea's Internet connections and IP addresses are depicted in Figure 7.

Photo Removed Due to Copyright Restrictions

Figure 7.   North Korea Internet Footprint (after APNIC, 2014).

The international community views North Korea as a underdeveloped state that is barely surviving with continuous humanitarian aid to provide them with food (Worden, 2008). This is not the case with their military. Their military continuously studies their adversaries' tactics to take full advantage of the enemy's weaknesses and capitalize on their strengths (Sang-ho, 2014a). Their military-first mentality and technology-forward attitude makes it unsurprising that they have and continue to develop their cyber capabilities. Since 2000, their late dictator Kim Jong II was advocating technological advances; he stated that there were three types of fools, one of them being computer illiterate people (Zemlianichenko, 2003). However, North Korea began developing its cyber capabilities since 1986 with the Pyongyang Informatics Center (Brown, 2004) and in the 1990's they established the Korean Computer Center (Carr, 2011). They have at least four units (Clarke & Knake, 2010) with anywhere between 100–12,000 members and a budget of 56 million dollars. The outcome of a 2005 South Korean simulation was that North Korea had the capability to cripple the U.S. Pacific Command and they were eighth in a cyber-threat ranking (Ventre, 2011). A listing of likely North Korean cyber organizations is given in Table 4. Additionally, analysts think that North Korea has cyber warriors stationed in other states that can carry out cyberattacks from there, states such as Japan and China (Carr, 2011; Clarke & Knake, 2010). This indicates that North-Korea-directed attacks could be originating from military members stationed overseas.

Photo Removed Due to Copyright Restrictions

Table 4.   North Korea Cyber Elements (after Brown, 2004; Clarke & Knake, 2010; Sang-Ho, 2014a).

In North Korea the division between the government and the private sector does not exist. The North Korean constitution clearly states that all organizations are state owned, such as banks, enterprises, major factories, communications, and education is state provided (Worden, 2008). Their technology research institutions work closely with their military to develop their cyber capabilities. They have seven technology research lab centers and academic institutions focused on cyber development (Brown, 2004). Libicki has also assessed DPRK cyber-warfare skills to parallel Iran's (cited in Sang-ho, 2014b). South Koreans believe North Korea has been gathering intelligence about computer systems and critical infrastructure in South Korea and has planned the best attack vector for each network infrastructure (Strategy Page, 2011). Considering all this information, it appears that the DPRK is a very capable cyber opponent as well as having knowledge of South Korea's cyber infrastructure. It is important to note that a DPRK-initiated cyberattack may not necessarily originate from DPRK territory due to the ease of spoofing and Internet North Korean cyber personnel out of the state (Sang-ho, 2014b).

C. NORTH-KOREA SUSPECTED CYBERATTACKS

It is important to establish attack vectors and a timeline of cyberattacks likely perpetrated by North Korea. South Korea has accused North Korea, as early as 2004, of being the perpetrator of various cyberattacks. All these cyberattacks were mostly against South Korean government, but they have also targeted civilian organizations, and coincided with political events such as the U.S. Independence day, ROK and U.S. exercises, and the Korean War anniversary. Either North Korea is the perpetrator or another state or non-state actor is timing their attacks to make it seem as if North Korea was committing these cyberattacks. When assessing North Korea's involvement, we have to take into account the motivation of the state involved; in this case, North Korea has been aggressive about taking actions against the South for anything they view as anti-DPRK. Also, North Korea has both the capability and skill to do cyberattacks. The following cyberattacks are noteworthy:

1.   July 2004

Over 270 South Korean government computers such as the Korea Atomic Energy were infected with a malware virus that could perform data exfiltration including passwords (Brockman-Hawe, 2007). According to Brockman-Hawe, the South Korea National Intelligence Center (NIS) declared this a North-Korea-conducted attack, whereas Brown (2004) stated that the NIS identified Chinese hackers as the perpetrators. However, it would not be out of the question for North Korea to buy viruses from Chinese hackers.

2.   August/September 2005

South Korea announced the discovery of North Korea's intrusion of 33 military communications sites during the annual Ulchi-Focus Lens Exercise with the United States (Ventre, 2011). Every year, North Korea condemns this exercise as preparation for attacks against the North and issues statements about conducting their own preemptive attacks or retaliation if the exercise goes on (Panda, 2014).

3.   July 2006

According to Ventre (2011), North Korea, specifically Unit 121, breached and damaged South Korean and U.S. Department of Defense servers.

4.   October 2007

North Korea apparently tested a 'logic bomb' cyber-weapon, and consequently the United Nations (UN) Security Council issued a resolution to ban computer imports to North Korea (Ventre, 2011). A logic bomb is an event-driven or time-driven piece of malware that will deploy once it is triggered (Schmitt, 2013). The UN sanctions were to prevent North Korea from obtaining the hardware and software to continue developing cyber weapons.

5.   September 2008

South Korea accused North Korea of sending emails to their military that contained Trojan horses (Ventre, 2011). Spear-phishing emails also targeted senior officials with names apparently provided by a previous North Korean defector suspected of still working for the North (Leyden, 2008).

6.   March 2009

North Korea was alleged to have stolen over 1,000 documents about hazardous material that contained secret information from the National Institute of Environmental Research, through an infected document transmitted via email (Ventre, 2011). It took seven months for South Korea to discover the implanted code on a computer belonging to a South Korean officer (Clarke & Knake, 2010). After initial penetration, the attackers obtained a password to access the South Korean Chemical Accidents and Response Information System to steal data (Raska, 2013). The long period until discovery increased the value of the data lost, the cost of responding to the attack, and the ability to assess the damages correctly.

7.   July 2009

A distributed-denial-of-service (DDoS) attack was conducted against 35 South Korean and U.S. government websites (Sang-ho, 2014a). The attack was conducted using botnets to send traffic to a targeted website list (Vlahos, 2014; Clarke & Knake, 2010). The NIS determined North Korean involvement, specifically Unit 110, because of the timing and sophistication of the attack (Clarke & Knake, 2010). The bot computers were found in 74 states, the masters in eight states, and the command and control in England (Clarke & Knake, 2010). Furthermore, there is evidence that the code was targeting the Korean language (Carr, 2011). Ventre (2011) judged the objective of this attack to be to test South Korea and U.S. resilience against this type of cyberattack.

8.   November 2009

North Korea was accused of stealing a plan that specified U.S. and South Korea strategy in case of a war with North Korea (Ventre, 2011). A South Korean officer initiated the attack when he used an infected universal serial bus drive and switched between classified networks and the Internet (Raska, 2013). Clarke & Knake state that the use of the Korean character set was discovered. North Korea is interested in war plans, which would give them the military advantage.

9.   January, March, and October 2010

More cases throughout 2010 of data exfiltration attacks involved targeting South Korean officers with malware. The targets included the South Korean Ministry of Defense and Foreign Affairs offices, and some of the documents stolen included information on China and North Korea relationship (Ventre, 2011). Aggressors used phishing attacks to set up an Advanced Persistent Threat (APT) and continued access to South Korean networks to conduct data exfiltration, while remaining undetected. An APT is a constant link between the attackers and the target to gather and extract information, install additional malware, or disrupt operations (Symantec, 1995).

10.   March 2011

A DDoS attack was conducted against South Korean banks through botnets. McAfee Labs assessed the attack as having North Korean signature, and the attack was similar to the 2009 attacks (Vlahos, 2014). McAfee (2011) discovered the use of Korean character sets in a white paper assessment of what they called "Ten Days of Rain." McAfee discovered that the code was similar, but more sophisticated, than the 2009 attacks, that it had a set timeframe for the attacks (10 days), contained a target list, deleted and overwrote files, and was set to damage the bot's master boot record (MBR) after completion of the attack. This type of attack requires the OS, applications, and data to be rebuilt. As Carr (2011) has argued, if these were cyber criminals, they will want to continue using the bots instead of destroying them. Since these were nation-state actors that destroyed another state's systems and data, either the aggressor state or the individuals involved could be held accountable under international laws.

11.   June 2012

A South Korea citizen was arrested for selling infected online games that contained a virus to convert computers into bots once the game was played (Chul-jae & Gwang-lip, 2012). There were over 100,000 games run and the South Korean government was investigating a ROK citizen for suspicion of working with North Korea (Chul-jae & Gwang-lip, 2012). Chul-jae and Gwang-lip reported that the NIS had linked the ROK citizen to the DPRK's Reconnaissance General Bureau. This could be one of the links between North Korea and the attacks against South Korea, by indicating that North Korea may have been controlling the South Korean bots.

12.   June 2012

South Korean officials said North Korea was involved in the hacking and disabling of a South Korean newspaper (Lee, 2013). The JoonhAng Ilbo was targeted and their databases containing articles and photos were deleted (Myo-ja & Tae-hee, 2012). North Korea had previously threatened seven South Korean media organizations for their coverage of a Pyongyang event (Myo-ja & Tae-hee, 2012). The perpetrator attacked the server through an employee website (Myo-ja & Tae-hee, 2012). This is another instance of North Korea indiscriminately targeting a civilian organization.

13.   March 2013

South Korean banks' and broadcasting firms' computers systems were wiped completely by embedded malware (Sang-ho, 2014a). The attack was planned for eight months, perpetrated through an email attachment, and was said to involve six computers with North Korean IP addresses (Gallagher, 2013). The IP address 175.45.178.xx was observed during a brief moment (Kwang-tae, 2013); this IP address belongs to North Korea as depicted on Figure 7. Furthermore, Kim Seung-joo assessed that this was not only credible since it was an accidental IP exposure, but also suggests that North Korea is also the culprit in previous attacks (Kwang-tae, 2013). However, Vlahos (2014) claims that even though South Korea blamed North Korea, specialists discovered over 1,000 IP addresses located in different states. Nonetheless, the U.S. Federal Bureau of Investigation (FBI) (2014) has also announced North Korea as the perpetrator of this attack. This type of attack is another case of specifically targeting civilian organizations.

14. June 2013

A DDoS attack was conducted against South Korean government and commercial websites (Sang-hun, 2013). However, hackers apparently also targeted North Korea (Sang-hun, 2013). The South Korean investigators found similarities to the code used in March 2011 and concluded North Korea involvement by analyzing the code, IP addresses used, and linked to the significant Korean War anniversary date (Sang-hun, 2013). Investigators also assessed that the attackers planned the attack for months due to discovering the weak access points into the targets (Sang-hun, 2013).

15. November 2014

An attack was made against Sony Pictures Entertainment (SPE) in November 2014. SPE and movie theaters were threatened to stop movie distribution (FBI, 2014) of a satirical movie with the plot to murder the North Korean leader (FoxNews.com, 2015). This attack met its objective as it coerced SPE and movie theaters not to distribute the movie. The FBI attributed the attack to North Korea (FBI, 2014). SPE provided the FBI with "raw data" of the attack (FoxNews.com, 2015). The FBI took steps to establish attribution by correlating previously used signatures, algorithms, and IP addresses linked to North Korea. The FBI concluded that the cyberattack was destructive malware and that data theft included "proprietary information as well as employees' personally identifiable information and confidential communications" (FBI, 2014). FoxNews.com (2014) reported that the cyberattack disclosed private information, disrupted SPE, and destroyed data. The FBI added that "the attacks also rendered thousands of SPE's computers inoperable, forced SPE to take its entire computer network offline, and significantly disrupted the company's business operations."

Experts have estimated the damages of this cyberattack were from 70 million to 100 million dollars, and the cost includes investigations and computer repair and replacement (Richwine, 2014). A SPE executive lost her job due to damaging emails that were disclosed (Rushe, 2015). Additionally, the cyberattack damaged SPE's reputation and working relationships, and this could be worse than the financial damage. Intangible damage can be hard to measure. SPE has cyber insurance which will offset some of the cost; however, it can take up to six months to fully account for the damage of this cyberattack (Richwine, 2014). SPE reported that because of their cyber insurance, the attack only cost them 15 million dollars (Rushe, 2015). Richwine reports that SPE has an operating budget of over 500 million dollars, so the attack might not be significant for them. This would not be the case for organizations that have smaller budgets and can be placed out of business with a single cyberattack. This cyberattack makes a case for "cyber insurance"; but more importantly, it illustrates that nation-states can leverage cyberspace as a coercion tool to mandate actions from any entity, continue to target civilian organizations, and attack liberties afforded by a state such as privacy and freedom of speech. This attack is of particular importance because it showed that attribution could be established through malware authorship and attack origin. Even if this particular cyberattack is not considered an act of war, a nation-state targeted a civilian organization, which is a clear violation of international laws.

D. ATTRIBUTION ANALYSIS OF THE ATTACKS

Experts have looked at the similarities and differences of the most recent attacks against South Korea to determine code provenance and possible perpetrators. Seo, Won, and Hong (2011) analyzed the DDoS attacks against South Korea in July 2009 and in March 2011 by inspecting traffic initiated from infected systems during both of these incidents from the Pohang University of Science and Technology (POSTECH). The researchers assumed the malware had corrupted POSTECH systems, collected outgoing traffic during the attacks, and only analyzed suspicious traffic. They found the following similarities between the two incidents: (1) the attacks were autonomous with a predefined target list and start date and time; (2) they used botnets with low-rate (54.2kbs) attacks to remain undetected on the infected hosts; (3) they used multiple forms of DDoS attacks (TCP SYN floods, ICMP floods, UDP floods, and HTTP GET/POST flood); and (4) the bots included instructions to delete documents and corrupt the MBR. They discovered more sophistication in the March 2011 attack with the command and control used for modifying malware code to avoid newly implemented signatures. The malware also prevented the host antivirus software from receiving any antivirus updates, they encrypted communications to make analysis difficult, and the termination of the attacks could only be achieved through disabling the bot.

The U.S.-Computer Emergency Response Team (CERT) (2013) published analysis of the March 2013 attacks through code evaluation; they determined the code was designed to avoid South Korean antivirus signatures. According to the U.S.-CERT, the malware was targeting South Korea, it was designed to affect multiple operating systems, corrupt the MBR, delete files, and included specific dates and times for the attacks to commence. The U.S.-CERT assessed the code to be unsophisticated but still capable of causing high damage. The characteristics of this attack are very similar to the characteristics described by Seo et al., which points to the same attacker for all three events. FireEye analysts corroborate the U.S.-CERT assessments for this particular attack (Pidathala, Khalid, Singh, & Vashisht, 2013) and provide more in-depth analysis of the malware code. FireEye analysts indicate that after enumerating the system's files, the attackers replaced them with the Roman army words "Hastati" and "Princpes" and corrupted the MBR to make it unusable (Pidathala et al., 2013). The malware would also disable the South Korean antivirus by issuing a taskkill command for AhnLab software, produced by a popular South Korean antivirus software organization, and the malware would check the time to commence the attack at the specified time (Pidathala et al., 2013).

Dell SecureWorks Counter Threat Unit (CTU) also analyzed the wiper malware used during the March 2013 attacks against South Korea. In addition to the same discoveries made by FireEye analysts, the CTU found that the dropper code was not designed to propagate, but was to be dropped by another program, which could have been over HTTP as there was an increase of executable HTTP downloaded traffic a month before the attacks from the published IP addresses as shown on Figure 8 (Dell SecureWorks, 2013). This attack vector is particularly important as FireEye points to a North Korea modus operandi in their World War C report, which consists of hacking websites with malware to take over their OS and where malware is downloaded to disable their antivirus (Geers et al., 2013). AhnLab Security also found the malware code would generate new files that included script to destroy the systems' disk and MBR for the

64

attacks conducted on March 2013 (AhnLab, 2013). The malicious code would overwrite the /kernel, /usr, /etc, and /home directories with zeroes for Linux systems and for the windows systems physical drives 0–9 would be overwritten with PRINCPES (AhnLab, 2013). Additionally, AhnLab reported the malware code was polymorphic to continue evading detection such as changing the string "PRINCPES to "PR!NCPES" (AhnLab, 2013).

Photo Removed Due to Copyright Restrictions

Figure 8.   Timeline of executable file download events over HTTP
(from Dell SecureWorks, 2013).

McAfee assessed that the same group has been behind all the cyberattacks against South Korea since 2009. They believe the group's objective was espionage since the attacks only looked for military specific data before extraction; even though they could destroy the systems' boot loader since 2009, it was only used during the March 20, 2013 attacks (Sherstobitoff & Liba, 2013). Sherstobitoff and Liba concluded these attacks to be related because it is mostly the same code event using the same password for the zip files, with some added functionality over time such as being able to extract files in the later versions. Sherstobitoff and Liba also point that these attacks could have been perpetrated by the New Romanic Army Cyber Team because of their use of ancient Roman military terms; however, North Korea could also be using those strings to introduce doubt as to who the real perpetrators are. Symantec has also linked cyberattacks against South Korea since 2009 to include the June 2013 attack (Figure 9), and assessed the gang Dark Seoul as the perpetrators with financial and political support, intelligence and coordination, and some level of sophistication (Symantec, 2013).

Photo Removed Due to Copyright Restrictions

Figure 9.   Four years of Dark Soul (from Symantec, 2013).

It is evident that South Korea has been the target of these attacks because the attacks are not only pre-configured to run on historical dates, but they are designed to evade specific South Korean antivirus software, and the target list consists mainly of South Korean organizations and target military terms. The autonomous attacks prolonged the attacks and prevented South Korea from responding to the incidents quickly because it meant that every bot had to be stopped for the attacks to stop, which increased the cost associated with these attacks. Autonomous attacks also point to North Korea because they need to use attacks that do not require much command-and-control to execute because of their limited Internet connections. Most of the infected bots were in South Korea (Seo et al., 2011), which can also point to North Korea's involvement, as they have been involved in attempting to grow botnets in South Korea through methods such as infected games, phishing attacks, and HTTP executables. Carr (2011) also discusses a theory of cybercriminal involvement in creating the botnets, but the code's self-destruction characteristics made it unlikely because cybercriminals like to maintain control for future use instead of releasing the bots after a particular attack. The code also contained instructions to find specific military files for extraction, and these files were of special interest to North Korea. Moreover, the highlighted increased level of malware sophistication and added functions with each attack are expected improvements for organized military cyber units that continue developing their skills.

E.   ANALYSIS

South Korea is one of the most technologically advanced states in the world with a National Cyber Security Center, cyberwar unit, and 177 cyber training centers (Ventre, 2011). South Korea is also a member of the Asian Pacific-CERT (AP-CERT), which can provide emergency response aid (APCERT, 2005). South Korea is particularly susceptible to cyberattacks due to its Internet footprint; almost 85% of its population has an Internet connection as shown on Table 5. This means that releasing an untargeted cyberattack against South Korea's networks has a high percentage for collateral damage, or in other words, an attacker can expect the damage to the private sector to be extensive. The challenge of discrimination during a cyberattack is compounded by both military and civilian organizations using the same types of software and hardware, which makes targeted weapon deployment more difficult. Additionally, North Korea most likely cannot develop a carefully targeted cyberattack consistent with the Law of Armed Conflict (LOAC), since they have repeatedly targeted civilian organizations during previous attacks.

YEAR	ROK Population	ROK Internet Users	ROK % Pop Internet Users	DPRK Population	DPRK % Pop Internet Users
2001	47,177,811	26,702,641	56.60%	22,977,355	0
2003	47,656,631	31,215,093	65.50%	23,330,469	0
2005	48,005,157	35,283,790	73.50%	23,620,923	0
2007	48,250,148	38,021,116	78.80%	23,907,668	0
2009	48,508,972	39,583,321	81.60%	24,190,924	0
2011	48,754,657	40,836,900	83.76%	24,457,492	0
2013	48,955,203	41,499,325	84.77%	24,720,407	0

Table 5.   Percentage of Individuals Using the Internet-South Korea versus North Korea (after ITU, 2014; U.S. Census Bureau, 2013).

1. Damage Costs

It is safe to assume that the ROK can respond to cyberattacks with AP-CERT aid. Nevertheless, the cost for South Korea to assess the damage and impact of cyberattacks, rebuild affected systems, restore backup data, and conduct an investigation is significant. Hern (2013) reported that the cyberattacks against South Korea cost approximately 780 million dollars in 2013, 9 million dollars in 2011, and 49 million dollars in 2009. Another researcher (Park, 2010) used a different model to estimate the damage of these cyberattacks. His model calculated the damaged per organization instead of whole cost, and includes acquisition cost of any asset required to resolve the attack, operations cost, business-opportunity cost, and indirect cost in respect to any entity classification. He assess the cost for one agency with a 24 hour downtime to be over 380 thousand dollars. He also listed cost for the July 2004 cyberattacks against South Korea to be between 95 million and 1.5 billion dollars, and the July 2009 cyberattacks to between 32 and 50 million dollars.

South Korea conducted similar steps to find out the total cost of the many attacks they have endured. For example to assess one aspect of direct damage, South Korea had to scan all networks to find affected systems, determine vulnerabilities, contain the attacks, patch systems, and notify antivirus organizations to prevent further damage, which has to be performed by specialists. The National Institute of Standards and Technology notes that it can take several months to recover from significant cyberattacks (Cichonski, Millar, Grance, & Scarfone, 2012), adding to the overall cost of the attack. This recovery time can be devastating to an organization.

2. Establishing Attribution

The ability to use systems around the world complicates attribution, but it is not impossible. Attribution can be achieved through a combination of technical steps and recognition of significant political, historical, or other types of events. Attribution is necessary to request international aid with prosecution, recovery, and for compensation after a cyberattack occurs. Then forensic analysis will attempt to ascertain the possible attacker by establishing the attack vector, following the traversal path to the attack origin, and analyzing malware provenance by determining if the malware resembles other malicious code previously attributed to a state. The characteristics discovered and published by various researchers on the different attacks against South Korea strongly suggest that these attacks are related. Additionally, origin IP addresses linked to North Korea were discovered in previous attacks.

North Korea also has motivation to continue attacking South Korea through cyberspace. North Korea has conducted conventional attacks since the 1950's (Hae-in, 2011) to break United States and ROK ties and reunify the Koreas (Maxwell, 2013). The war between North and South Korea has never officially ended, and cyberspace has provided North Korea with another avenue of approach to keep harassing the South at a relatively low cost. North Korea will lose if a kinetic war were to occur because of support by U.S. military power. In cyberspace, North Korea can continue to attack South Korea's financial institutions, private organizations, and military without having to use many resources and with the ability to hide behind plausible deniability (Sang-ho, 2014a). Furthermore, no one has held North Korea responsible for the past attacks so they have no fear of reprisal.

Even with all these facts, we must also consider if other states might be the culprits of the attacks on South Korea. What would another state gain by making North Korea seem as the perpetrator of the attack or by assisting them? Other states that might be able to conduct these types of cyberattacks are China and Russia; they are aware of the strong partnership between South Korea and the United States and may not want to attack the United States directly. Even if China is not the culprit, it might be at least an abettor, as North Korea's Internet connections are routed through China as reflected in Figure 7 (APINIC, 2014). So, it is possible that China could be responsible for the attacks or abetting North Korea in retaliation for the United States' current lawsuit against the five officers of Unit 61398 who conducted cyberespionage against U.S. organizations (U.S. Department of Justice, 2014). It could also be Russia in an attempt to keep the United States occupied in another part of the world and give them freedom of maneuver in Europe. If South Korea traced the attacks to either of these states, these states would know exactly who was behind the attacks due to their highly controlled connections; it would be almost impossible for perpetrators to be in these states and their government not be aware of their cyber activities (Clarke and Knake, 2010). We must also take in consideration that once a state uses a cyber-weapon, antivirus companies and other technology organizations are able to develop attack signature and add it to intrusion detection and protection mechanisms to stop it from causing any more damage, rendering that cyber-weapon unusable in the future. Thus Russia and China have more to lose than to gain from using North Korea as a scapegoat and releasing cyber weapons in their arsenal.

The established links between the attacks and significant events point to North Korea as the most likely perpetrator of these cyberattacks. DPRK military organizations are the predominant users of computer systems in North Korea. North Korea has also set a pattern of their persistence and ability to leverage different types of cyberattacks against South Korea. North Korea can also be found liable due to North Korea's control of the private sector: The attack can be established as state-executed, which Healy (2011) described as national government conducting "the attack using cyber forces under their direct control" (p. 2). With an international acceptable level of attribution to North Korea, North Korea should have to make restitutions per international law and jus post bellum.

3.   Cyberattack Responses

Even though North Korea is a "rogue state" that ignores international law, South Korea could force North Korea to repay them damages through sanctions, and could enlist the help of other states to also sanction North Korea. Sanctions are more successful when multiple states enforce them against belligerents. South Korea can invoke Article 39, 41, and 42 of the UN Charter (1945) and present all the collected evidence to the UN Security Council to force them to take action against North Korea. Under Article 39, the council will evaluate the evidence and determine if "the existence of any threat to the peace exits, breach of the peace, or act of aggression" and "what measures shall be taken in accordance with Article 41 and 42." South Korea will need to let the UN Security Council attempt to settle the dispute without the use of an armed force under Article 41, such as by economic sanctions, and only after failure to stop the threat, will the UN

Security Council allow South Korea to use military operations to maintain or restore peace under Article 42. Sanctions against a state with nothing to lose will probably not reach the sanctions' objective and South Korea will be forced to respond through other actions.

Responding to cyberattacks involves a significant amount of time and resources and requires response personnel to have technical knowledge. Some private organizations in South Korea may be unfit to face the attacks and end up bankrupt. Therefore, South Korea can also formally bring matters against North Korea through the International Court of Justice (ICJ), as they are also responsible for protecting states and enforcing customary international law (ICJ, 2015). The ICJ can then review the evidence, conduct investigations, and issue their ruling, which North Korea, as a signatory of the UN Charter, is mandated to abide by (ICJ, 2015). Even a single attack can be sufficiently damaging that the perpetrators should be held accountable and pay the monetary damages. That is, the ICJ can enforce tort law, which stipulates that if an aggressor conducts an intentional act to cause harm, the victim can pursue a lawsuit to obtain compensation; cyberspace torts are classified as intentional torts (Grama, 2010). North Korea has intentionally harmed private entities through cyberspace therefore; they should compensate South Korea for the damages they have incurred. The more state –on-state cyberattacks become prevalent, the more the UN and ICJ will need to set precedents to prosecute states that do not act within international laws.

South Korea can try to coerce North Korea to stop attacking them by launching a counterattack. South Korea should try to show North Korea that they not only have the knowledge of the intricacies of their intranet, but they can also cause them some serious damage if they choose to, since air-gapped system do not get updated often and have persistent vulnerabilities. Libicki (2013) argues that the brittleness of enemy systems can be demonstrated by the ability to hack into enemy systems at any time. A show of force may help coerce North Korea to sign agreements promising compensation and to cease any future cyberattacks against South Korea.

Can South Korea abide by the basic principles of the law of armed combat in a cyber response to North Korea? The basic principles of LOAC are distinction, proportionality, military necessity, and humanity (Carr, 2011). Only a few top-level government officials in North Korea have access to the Internet (Ventre, 2011;Sang-ho, 2014a). Moreover, "only a fraction of the 25 million citizens are allowed to use tightly controlled intranets" (Sang-ho, 2014a). Consequently, targeted cyberattacks on North Korean computer systems will be a direct attack on their military and government systems, which will abide by the principle of distinction of only targeting combatants. The attack will also meet the proportionality criteria, as the attack should not exceed the use of force to achieve the results sought. This attack will also meet the military necessity criteria, as the cyberattack will seek to only "weaken the military forces of the enemy" (ICRC, 2002, p. 7). Additionally, such attacks can be consistent with the humanity principle because they can avoid unnecessary suffering and injuries with a reversible cyberattack.

F.   CONCLUSION

The DPRK and the ROK are still at war so cyberattacks conducted by North Korea need to abide by LOAC. As Schmitt (2013) stated about the Georgia 2008 cyberattacks, any cyberattacks that are part of hostilities should be governed by LOAC. North Korea has demonstrated their inability or unwillingness to abide by the principles of international law and continue violating South Korea's sovereignty by crossing into their borders, making civilian organizations and infrastructure primary targets, incurring significant collateral damage, and incurring damaging economic effects. It is also clear that DPRK Government organizations conducted the attacks, which means the North Korean government should be held accountable for these actions.

South Korea does have the technical expertise to deal with these major cyberattacks, but it has cost them millions of dollars to respond and clean up after them. We should be concerned about states that lack the capability or capital to respond to cyberattacks of this scale. Additionally, since the level of sophistication for cyberattacks will continue to increase, as McAfee labs determined from the 2009 to 2011 against South Korea, the fact that we have not seen a lethal cyberattack does not mean that it is impossible.

Since we know North Korea has repeatedly attacked South Korea, the UN, through the ICJ, can subpoena packet information between these two states to facilitate accountability after a cyberattack, and those third-party states that refuse to cooperate can be "suspected of being involved in the attack" (Rowe, 2015). The UN will need international cooperation to obtain information from the different traversed routers. The level of attribution should be sufficient for the UN, the ICJ, and other states to collectively respond. Nonetheless, various factors shape UN actions in the Korean Peninsula and limit their ability to respond to the cyberattacks perpetrated by North Korea, such as the tasks of controlling problems that could easily escalate or deteriorate. Some examples of these problems are the possibility of war in the Korean Peninsula, maintaining peace talks, handling North Korea's established military objective to reunite the Koreas, and addressing North Korea's inability to feed their citizens without international aid (Worden, 2008). There are also complex relationships between the DPRK, the ROK, and the United States because of mistrust. This complicates response actions, such as South Korea and the United States not conducting annual exercises or promising aid in response to North Korea's assurance to stop nuclear weapon proliferation and missiles exports, although North Korea has not abided with such agreements (Worden, 2008). However, previous attacks showed that if state-sponsored attacks continued to go unpunished, civilian organizations will continue to be targeted. The SPE hack was an example because the FBI not only publicly attributed the cyberattack to a state, but the United States also issued sanctions against North Korea. The global community needs more cases like this to hold belligerents accountable either through sanctions or tort law.

THIS PAGE INTENTIONALLY LEFT BLANK

VI. RECOMMENDATIONS

A. CYBER-WARFARE JUS POST BELLUM FRAMEWORK

This study argues for a cyber-post-conflict framework. Some International Humanitarian Law (IHL) conventions and treaties certainly apply to cyber-warfare post-conflict, but they fall short in other areas. For example, the Hague Conventions mandate that states provide recovery assistance or restitution for cultural property at the conclusion of an armed conflict, and they prohibit the use of neutral powers to conduct attacks (ICRC, 2014), so damage to neutral states will need to be repaired post bellum. Respecting neutral states is difficult for a cyber-weapon deployment through the Internet, as it must traverse many boundaries to reach its target; the best way to respect neutrality is to release cyber weapons only against air-gapped systems through removable media or interference with supply chains.

The lack of cyber-warfare specific laws affects jus post bellum because it limits states' ability to seek international aid to prosecute violations and mandate compensation. Guns for hire in cyberspace are not currently covered by international law. Conventions for Certain Conventional Weapons (CCW) prohibit indiscriminate and excessive effects (ICRC, 2014), so conventions for cyber weapons can be established that outline specific limitations and prohibitions. The IHL conventions were written in the late 1800's and early 1900's (ICRC, 2014), so the wording poorly applies to cyberspace operations. Even the additions of the various conventions in 1977 do not sufficiently cover cyberspace since no one foresaw that the Internet would become central to both civilian and military operations. Nonetheless, we can propose the following framework to address cyber post-conflict.

1. Outlaw Unethical Cyber Weapons

The first step is to discourage proliferation of unethical cyber weapons by holding states accountable post bellum when jus in bello violations occur. Ethical weapons include weapons that their only intent is to meet their objective and then self-destruct, precise cyber weapons, cyber weapons that will have less collateral damage than a kinetic

75

attack (Denning and Strawser, 2014), and reversible attacks (Rowe, 2010). Giesen (2013), Rowe et al. (2011), Denning and Strawser (2014), and Liaropolous (2010) agree that unethical cyber weapons should not be used to obtain military objectives. A new convention, such as those for CCWs, can satisfy this.

The International Committee of the Red Cross should be the lead for establishing such cyber weapons conventions since they are overseers of IHL (ICRC, 2002). The convention would ban any weapon in violation of current established laws and will include new stipulations and punishment for indiscriminate weapons or state sponsored cyberattacks strictly targeting civilians, as well as address the shortfalls of current international laws in cyberspace. The new convention for cyber-weapon development and proliferation would seek to stop the use of immoral cyber weapons and encourage only the development of ethical cyber weapons, with the understanding that there might be occasions where the use of a cyber-weapon will be more ethical.

It will not be an easy task, but the onus falls on the cyber warriors that will need to avoid development of indiscriminate cyber weapons and follow operations planning and targeting process to vet and validate legal targets, methods of attack, and conduct proper battle damage assessment to avoid overkill. Cyber operators must be able to determine if the deployed weapon will meet the desired effects and determine cascading effects to inform the decision makers of the consequences of deploying a cyber-weapon. Iasiello (2004) advocates for safeguarding the innocent; a convention for cyber weapons will help protect the innocent and avoid unnecessary suffering due to deployment of cyber weapons.

2. Add Critical Cyber Infrastructure to the Protected Sites

Cyber weapons can target anything in cyberspace. Because of the dual use and interconnectedness of civilian and military cyber-infrastructure, critical cyber infrastructure should be added to the protected sites to protect civilians from the ravages of war and keep states accountable for their actions in cyberspace.

Article 50 and 56 of Additional Protocol I to the Geneva Conventions of 1949 (1977) try to afford more protection to civilians and civilian infrastructure. Article 50 and

57 prohibit attacks that may cause "damage to civilian objects" and article 56 protects sites against attacks that may have serious consequences for civilians. However, these articles do not correctly address cyberspace because Article 56 is meant for infrastructure that would expel dangerous forces and, as Jakobson (2011) states, some cyberattacks may not have any physical damage. Essentially, these articles are not enough protection for critical cyber infrastructure. Therefore, this thesis endorses Geib and Lahmann (2012) in recommending establishment of a humanitarian "safe heaven" in cyberspace that would include any cyber infrastructure that has significant civilian purpose. They propose that states should only target dual-use targets with reversible attacks. There are a variety of reversible attacks that can be used, such as those proposed by Rowe (2010) against dual-use targets. The reversible attacks would avoid wide spread destruction and make reconstruction easier for both victor and defeated. The protection of cyber critical infrastructure and outlining methods of attack for dual-use systems would ensure cyber weapon deployments avoid targeting cyber infrastructure by any means that could cause excessive and unnecessary suffering.

3. International Community Involvement

There can be many entities involved in post bellum activities and reconstruction, since it will be difficult for all but the most powerful states to accomplish all post bellum activities from cyber-warfare alone. To successfully assign attribution and recover, there need to be international cooperation and aid agreements to facilitate investigations, keep states accountable, and provide recovery aid. Ferwerda et al. (2010) noted that there are still shortfalls with cooperation and links between the different international cyber-response units. An international organization solely responsible for dealing with international cyberattacks, which can coordinate cooperation, run relief efforts, and set priorities will ensure a fast response to cyberattacks and limit human suffering.

This thesis proposes that such an organization should be under the United Nations (UN), as they have the prosecution capability and they are responsible for ensuring peace between states (UN, 1945). The International Telecommunications Union currently provides a link between the UN and other cyber organizations (Ferweda et al., 2010), but it does not currently provide cyberattack recovery aid. The UN has precedents in creating organizations that protect humanity where no other boundaries exist such as the World Meteorological Organization, a specialized agency of 191 members that handles international cooperation for meteorological information (WMO, 2015).

A cyberwar-focused organization can be the lead for establishing cooperation agreements, leveraging existing international organizations, setting response actions, and sharing information. Information sharing could expedite antivirus responses to protect vulnerable systems. International cooperation will also ensure that lessons learned from each incident are tracked and not repeated, such as Iasiello's (2004) lessons learned recommendation. Additionally, a collective effort by an international organization can help a population recover post-conflict, as evidenced by the many organizations that were involved during the Kosovo and Iraq Wars. Having a single international organization will ensure that plans and priorities are set to avoid repetitive efforts, such as were encountered in Kosovo (Dursun-Ozkanca, 2009). Reconstruction includes many activities. States lacking technical knowledge will require even more aid for recovery and investigations. For example, Casey (2011) describes a system administrator that mistakenly overwrote some files during forensic analysis.

4. Accountability

Cyberattacks that frequently go unpunished would encourage more cyber actors to attacks without regard to established laws. Schmitt (2013) agrees that "a state bears international legal responsibility" for any attributable cyber action in violation of international rules (p. 29). Therefore, this thesis recommends a three-prong approach to enforcing accountability in cyberspace: punishment, restoration actions, and proportionality.

a. Punishment

Punishment would require attribution, which international cooperation agreements could facilitate. Orend (2007), Iasiello (2004), and Boon (2005) advocate for ensuring states are accountable for their actions during war. In the same way, the international community should hold states accountable for violating international laws in cyberspace.

Punishment can include monetary compensation and prosecution, which can be facilitated by the UN, the International Court of Justice, and the International Criminal Court. Punishments will begin deterring other cyber actors. Making states accountable for their actions in cyberspace would serve as a deterrent to reckless cyberattacks and would encourage ethical cyber weapons. Examples of punishment for deterrence are the five Chinese officers that have been charged for targeting American civilian organizations (U.S. Department of Justice, 2014) and the sanctions against North Korea because for the Sony Entertainment Pictures hack (FoxNews.com, 2015).

b.   *Restoration of Affected System and Infrastructure*

Orend (2007), Bass (2004), and Iasiello (2004) advocate for international reconstruction efforts. Bass specifically addresses restoring the economy and infrastructure. Orend recommends economic restitution on top of reconstruction aid, and Iasiello recommends a combined reconstruction effort by the victor and the defeated. Bass stipulates that victors should depart immediately unless a victim state does not have the technical means to recover. All these stipulations should also apply in cyberspace. The international community should ensure the responsible states provide support to the victims of their cyber weapon deployments. Nonetheless, lack of attribution does not clear the international community from collectively helping a state recover from a cyberattack.

c.   *Proportionality*

Orend (2007) tries to define fair peace settlements and Kant (2006) stipulates that peace agreements with ulterior motives would result in more hostilities. Boon (2005) advocates for having the ability to assess the level of intervention that is required. Therefore, proportionality in peace agreements will be important to ensure that the responses that both victor and defeated must undertake to resolve the conflict are fair, or otherwise the settlement will only be postponing an inevitable war. Proportionality also means that states and the international community involvement should not be excessive to the required need of the state to recover.

5. Plans

Post bellum plans should be considered before a cyber-weapon is deployed. Not having a post-bellum plan can lead to problems as the 2003 Iraq War demonstrated (McCready, 2009). Orend, Iasiello, and McCready advocate having post-bellum plans before the conflict concludes. This is especially important given the uncertainty of cyberattacks. Planning should include contingency operations, such as actions for cyber weapons that had unexpected and excessive collateral damage.

Each part of this framework mutually supports each other. We cannot hold states accountable for their action in cyberspace if there are no laws prohibiting those actions. The international community can then enforce accountability or discourage states from building unethical cyber weapons through punishments and mandating compensation. Additionally, an international organization will have to oversee compliance or states will not abide by the new established laws.

B. CYBERATTACK RESPONSE

A standard set of procedures would aid states to follow the same steps to resolve cyber post-conflict. The new UN cyber organization can establish such standards and procedures. Steps that can be used when responding to a cyberattack are shown in Figure 10 including steps to ensure attribution and accountability. As Casey (2011) points out, evidence must be properly handled and tracked, if charges are to stand up in an international court.

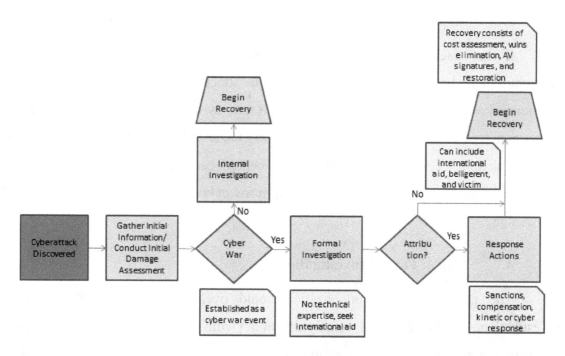

Figure 10.   Cyberattack Response Flowchart.

1.   Step 1: Information Gathering

Gather initial information and conduct initial damage assessment: The affected organization would gather pertinent attack information such as the attack type, the possible target, how long the attack has been going on, affected systems, and the impact of the attack. Organizations lacking technical knowledge can reach the national and regional cyber response centers to aid them in conducting this step.

2.   Step 2: Cyberwar

Establish whether the activity is cyberwar or not: This affects response actions. Even if the attack is not considered an act of war, the victim can still seek international aid. Categorizing the attack can determine if just-war theory is applicable. The attack can be categorized as unintentional, criminal, or a cyber act of war. If it was an unintentional incident, the state can begin the recovery phase immediately. If it was a criminal attack, then the state can attempt to identify the criminals and bring them to justice through either national or international cyber crime laws.

3. Step 3: International Notification

If the attack is an act of war, then the state should notify the international community and determine a response action. If the attack was not an act of war, it can be categorized as a criminal act, and the victim and state cyber organizations can conduct an investigation to establish attribution to a state, organization, or individual, and determine response actions. National and regional cyber centers can aid during investigations and during the recovery if the victim does not have cyber insurance or lacks technical knowledge.

4. Step 4: Formal Investigation

The new UN cyber organization could oversee or assist with a formal investigation. The international community and victim organizations can conduct the investigation ensuring proper procedures and chains of custody to ensure investigation outcomes are legitimate. If the victim state does not possess technical knowledge, the international organizations can support investigations and damage assessments. During the formal investigation, a damage assessment that includes direct, indirect, and any other type of effect should be conducted. The outcome of the investigation should specify some level of attribution.

5. Step 5: Attribution

Attribution can be established to a state, individual, or organization through technical steps and significant political, historical, or other events. Finding out if the attack was state-sponsored can be difficult as governments can use botnets, criminal entities, patriot hackers, or other cyber actors to invoke plausible deniability. But states that want a political effect, like North Korea, or Russia against Georgia in 2008, are not good at concealing the origins of their attacks. The victim state can seek international aid, such as from the UN and Computer Emergency Response Teams, to conduct the formal investigations. This would be especially beneficial for those states without the technical ability to conduct an investigation. The UN can then facilitate the investigation through international agreements, sanctions, and subpoenas to attempt to determine the aggressor and seek justice by holding the responsible individual or state accountable for their actions.

The attribution must be credible to the international community and be provable in court without revealing secrets. States can still establish a certain level of attribution without having to reveal how the attribution was made. Attribution does not have to be definite to be valid. For example, if the attack is traced to an organization within a state and the state refuses to investigate that organization because the attack was conducted on their behalf, then the state should be considered responsible for aiding and abetting aggressors.

6.   Step 6: Cyberattack Response

If attribution was established, responses can be in the form of prosecution, mandated compensation, and or sanctions. The punishment must fit the crime and appropriate punishment should set precedents for deterring other cyber actors.

7.   Step 7: Recovery

It could take a victim months to recover from a significant cyberattack (Cichonski et al, 2012). Therefore, this step has multiple sub-steps as it entails various actions to resolve a cyberattack and it can be resource-intensive. The victim and international community can conduct recovery. One of the questions for the international community is to assess if the attacked state has the technological capabilities and knowledge to resolve cyberattacks. Some states do not possess the necessary technical knowledge to restore systems, and would need more outside help to return systems to normal and ensure the attack has been contained. In some cases such as encryption attacks, the cyber-aggressor may need to supply key information about the attack to save time. The UN cyber organization can also coordinate agreements between the victim and belligerent to ensure conflict resolution.

a.   *Cost Assessment*

The state should find out as much information about the attack as possible to help them determine cost, such as making a list of affected systems, what information was taken and or deleted, what are the consequences of the lost information, and whether the systems have backups available. Some organizations have developed checklists to help targeted organizations determine cyberattack cost, such as Booz Allen Hamilton Incorporated (2014), Ponemon Institute (2013), and National Institute of Standards and Technology (Cichonski et al., 2012). These checklists can aid organizations enumerate damages and collect all pertinent information after a cyberattack. Checklists are helpful because assessing the damage of a cyberattack can encompass many elements and take time. Figure 11 gives an example. It includes direct, indirect, and other associated costs, which can be zero for costs that do not apply, such as for systems that do not contain any intellectual property.

Different factors can affect the cost of each section. For instance, the restoring of data can be affected by the volume of the data and connection and processor speeds. Appendix B shows a hypothetical filled-out checklist for a small organization and suggests how an organization can put out of business by one single costly cyberattack. The checklist in Figure 11 also suggests the significant actions that organizations must take to respond to attacks and assess the damage. This shows the difficulty a military organization would have when trying to do damage assessment after a cyber-weapon attack.

Photo Removed Due to Copyright Restrictions

Figure 11.   Cyberattack Cost Checklist
(after Booz Allen Hamilton Inc., 2014; and PI, 2013).

b.   *Vulnerabilities Elimination*

The victim would have to determine the type of attack and vector used to determine and eliminate the exploited vulnerabilities from their systems. Examples of vectors are an advanced persistent threat or malware through a zero-day vulnerability, removable media, malicious insider, or social engineering. The victim would have to scan all networks to identify affected systems and determine if the cyberattack has been contained or if it is still spreading. After the victim finds the vulnerability, the victim will have to develop a fix or replacement code to cure the affected systems. This may include disabling compromised accounts, patching, changing firewall rules, and changing passwords (Cichonski et al., 2012).

c.   *Anti-malware Signatures*

The victim will then have to create antivirus signatures to prevent any other systems from being affected by the same cyberattack. These will most likely be created by vendors and added to their vulnerability signature list. The antivirus vendors can then distribute the signature to other organizations to ensure other systems are protected from future damage because of that particular attack. International cooperation can help protect global system against similar attacks.

d.   *Restoration*

Backups of software and data are important for cyberattack responses because the easiest recovery involves restoring damaged software and data from backups. Restoration would be impossible if backups are not available, damaged, or not conducted correctly. Otherwise, software may be recovered from vendors or may have to be completely rebuilt (Cichonski et al., 2012). These recovery actions take time and resources.

e.   *Incident Response Planning*

Since computer systems are going to be susceptible to cyberattacks and states heavily rely on computer networks, government and at-risk organizations must have a recovery plan that includes data backup to facilitate restoration. Organizations that have detailed incident-response plans, such as tested backup files and response steps for different types of incidents, will do better under attack (Cichonski et al., 2012). Potential victims should also be concerned with making changes to prevent future attacks by either policy or infrastructure (Cichonski et al., 2012). The victim should review the incident response plans to find out what went wrong and prevent future attacks. If those plans do not already exist, the victim should seek to develop incident response plans that will enable fast incident handling.

f.   ***Education***

Education can help prevent future cyberattacks. International, regional, and national cyber organizations need to foster education for their users to prevent attacks

THIS PAGE INTENTIONALLY LEFT BLANK

VII. CONCLUSION

A. SUMMARY

International treaties and conventions do not sufficiently cover jus post bellum actions and various specialists recommended an addition of a third pillar to just war theory to properly address post-conflict activities (Stanh, 2008; Douglas, 2003; Orend, 2007; Iasiello, 2004; Österdahl 2012). Douglas argues that the lack of attention to jus post bellum can result in more hostilities, which was certainly the case during the Iraq War recovery period (McCready, 2009). It has been difficult to conduct post bellum actions during kinetic wars and now that we face a new warfighting domain in cyberspace, it will be even more difficult to apply international laws to cyber post-conflict situations. This study found that current International Humanitarian Law and international treaties and conventions do not sufficiently cover post-bellum issues. Analysis has been done on international law before and during a cyber conflict (Schmitt, 2013; Dörmann, 2001; Koh, 2012), as well as the effects of deployed cyberattacks against various states (Kaska et al., 2010). However, in the aftermath of a deployed cyber weapon; there is no formal mechanism for the assignment of accountability for the restoration of affected infrastructure and recovery from damages.

The increased cyberattacks against civilian organizations highlights the need for international agreements focused on cyber jus post bellum since civilians will share a disproportionate collateral damage from cyber warfare. Cyber-weapon deployment can have detrimental economic, physical, and psychological effects and extensive collateral damage. In addition, cyber-weapon effects are difficult to predict and they limit the ability to conduct damage assessment compared to conventional attacks, preventing the ability to assess their success rate. Another major problem in cyberspace is attribution, which affects accountability and response actions. Therefore, establishing attribution to assign accountability is essential in dealing with the aftermath of cyberattack. Attribution is not impossible, as significant events and forensic actions can establish some level of attribution that would be acceptable for international action. Attribution has been demonstrated by the United States charging the five Chinese officers (U.S. Department of

Justice, 2014) and issuing sanctions against North Korea in response for the Sony Pictures Entertainment hack (FoxNews.com, 2015), whether North Korea accepted culpability or not.

Jus post bellum is still important even when we cannot exactly identify the guilty party, as various organizations aid suffering states during post-conflict by clearing mines and providing food (Schmickle & Writer, 2003) even when they were not part of the conflict. For instance, there has been a collective effort to clear landmines around the world because they continue to claim innocent victims and prevent reconstruction efforts (U.S. Department of State, 1994). Just as there was a collective response for the 2003 Iraq and 1998 Kosovo Wars recovery, there also needs to be a collective cyber response after a cyberattack. These two wars showed various states and organizations involved in the recovery process and taking part in different actions to stabilize the state. Helping a state recover after a cyberattack can provide added benefits, such as gaining the trust of the victim's public and providing the supporting agency with first-hand attack insight which could enable discovering new vulnerabilities thereby protecting other systems against similar attack, which ultimately aids the global community. There are already established international organizations to aid with recovery after cyber conflict. However, to avoid the issues faced during the Kosovo and Iraq Wars, there needs to be a lead agency that has a recovery plan, aids in conducting proper assessments, coordinates recovery efforts, avoids duplicate actions, and establishes priorities.

Cyberattacks are not going away. There are similarities between kinetic and cyberwars, but there are also many differences. Additionally, international treaties and conventions were written to deal with conventional wars. Nonetheless, ideas introduced by theologists, scholars, ethicists, and specialists can be used to recommend to the international community ways to expand current international agreements or create new international agreements to prohibit unethical cyber weapons, safeguard cyber critical infrastructure, and establish proper behavior during the aftermath of cyber-weapon deployments.

There are already examples of international cooperation and international organizations that can facilitate the expansion or creation of new treaties and global organizations, such as the World Meteorological Organization, the International Telecommunication Union, and the Council of Europe Cybercrime Treaty. The lack of a global cyber emergency response center poses a problem. There should be a United Nations (UN) institution or another type of impartial third party global institution that oversees cyberspace, since "there is a marked absence of integrated global institutional mechanisms designed to track, record and respond to cyber incidents" (Ferwerda et al., 2010, p. 2). Investigations can then be facilitated by the new established body, so that belligerents cannot pretend the accusations are just fabrications from the attacked state. Additionally, attackers must not only be held accountable, but should also have the moral and ethical obligation to ensure restitutions are made. If states continue to conduct cyber-warfare freely without any consequences, more and more states may want to join in. Therefore, this study recommends international conventions for cyber post-conflict headed by the International Committee of the Red Cross as well as the establishment of a UN cyber organization that supervises state actions through cyberspace, ensures accountability, and sets procedures for dealing with the aftermath of a cyberattack.

B. FUTURE WORK

This study highlighted the difficulty of conducting damage assessments, especially for cyber military operations. Cyber battle damage assessments (BDA) methods, both technical and procedural, need to be made more specific. The Joint Targeting publication outlines BDA, but it does not specifically address cyber BDA (DOD, 2013), which leaves cyber warriors and decision makers with the difficult task of figuring how to correctly conduct BDA.

This study recommends the establishment of a UN cyber organization that would be responsible for setting polices and procedure for cyberspace, encouraging cooperation, and ensuring accountability. A study on the organization's structure would be helpful for the international community and can facilitate cooperation between the already established cyber organizations.